The ROADS of LIFE

The ROADS of LIFE

A MEMOIR OF FAMILY, MONTANA, AND ENJOYING THE JOURNEY

VERNON PETERSEN

Printed in the United States of America.
First paperback edition November 2022.

Cover and layout design by G Sharp Design, LLC.
www.gsharpmajor.com

Editing by Eland Mann.
www.ElandMann.com

ISBN 979-8-98713-630-0(paperback)
ISBN 979-8-98713-631-7 (ebook)

TABLE OF CONTENTS

A WORD FROM THE AUTHOR

THE IMPETUS FOR this book was primarily my two daughters encouraging me to do so. They wanted my childhood memories along with my occupational experiences. I had three major careers, some of which required me to address large audiences. I wrote all my own material, most of which intentionally included humor. The stories in this book all have enough truth to generate the subject, but many have been embellished to make them humorous and readable. So, although the book was written as a sort of documentary of my life, I believe you will enjoy the journey with me.

It is my belief that humor bridges many a divide amongst people of all walks of life, whether the divides are political or by age or race or occupation or any other differences—as long as the humor is self-deprecating. The story of my childhood days, I think, would be quite boring without some humor thrown in, which I have attempted to do in the following pages.

I hope this book will also show what a humble beginning, with the outstanding support and the hardworking role models my parents were, that living up to their standards—and with the Grace of God— can take you as far as you want to go in life. At least in the era that my life has spanned that was the case and I believe it is still today judging by our children and their successes in life. Much of that credit goes to my wonderful wife Dana. She was the stay-at-home role model and got the kids to church regularly which gave them the basics and morals of a Christian life.

We have four children: one is a computer programmer, one is an accounts payable team lead in a corporate office, one is a former chemical engineer and now a pharmacist, and one is a Baptist minister serving as a missionary in Uganda, East Africa, since 2000.

All of them are parents now so we have eleven grandchildren, nine of which have college degrees or are still in college. The other two are doing well without finishing college.

Much of this book takes place on roads. Dirt, gravel, graded—I've been down them all. Sometimes in a beat-up ranch truck, other times atop a Caterpillar bulldozer. If there's one thing I've learned from going down so many roads, it's this: making a go of life ain't easy, but family and a sense of humor can get you a long way. We never know where exactly the roads of life take us—and that's part of the fun.

THE ROADS OF YOUTH

CHAPTER 1
AN INAUSPICIOUS BEGINNING

I, VERNON LEE Petersen, was born on a blustery early winter day the 12th of November 1943 in a converted one room log schoolhouse about ten miles southwest of Sand Springs, Montana. My mother Alice Alvina Barker Petersen (1919-1983) and my grandmother Ina Rothwell Barker (1899-1995) were present for the occasion. My grandfather Emil Barker (1884-1962) was somewhere on the place working but not present until that night. My oldest brother Larry remembers the location differently as he thought I was born in the new house. So, I can't be sure but I remember Mom telling me the first version. Doesn't really matter I guess at this point.

After several days of recovery my dad, Carl Vernon Petersen (1919-2010), came with a team and wagon to take us home. I was then the youngest of their three sons, Larry Bruce, two years old, and Donald Milton, one year old. Home then was a one room dugout with a dirt floor in the side of a coulee about nine miles due west of Sand Springs. No electricity or water, just a wood stove and a log front with a door and a log roof covered with dirt.

So here was my mom with two toddlers and an infant to care for while Dad was gone on horseback almost all days watching over several hundred of his boss's yearling cattle. Besides her care of us she had to hand pump water to a wooden tank for some of the cattle. I developed pneumonia after the first of the year (1944) so she had that to deal with as well without any way of getting medicine or health care. I'm glad I don't remember any of that but I marvel at the stamina and pure grit that it took for them and us to survive.

That spring when the frost went out one of the yearlings wandered out onto the dirt roof and fell through and came down inside. As you might imagine the steer was a little startled so, as I understand it, he didn't just stand there waiting for someone to open the door. He instead went in search of an escape route in the tiny room on his own, so what was not damaged from the entry was put in disarray in the aftermath.

I'm not sure where we went in the meantime but I know Dad took a different job down on the Musselshell River where he remodeled a one-room chicken house that we then moved into. I think it was here that Larry tells a story about Donny and I. Mom had a large cardboard box that she used as a crib for me. One day Donny slid a chair over by it, crawled upon it, leaned over into the box and started tickling me. I, in response, got two hands full of his hair and began squealing and pulling which caused Donny to try to pull back, which exasperated the worsening situation. Larry ran outside and found Mom and he said she was finally able to break my grasp and release him. I don't remember that, but I also don't remember Donny ever tickling me, so maybe he did remember.

Larry Vernon Donald (Donny)

There was also an annual event that us boys dreaded and feared. It was the tick shot and the annual chest x-ray. The tick shot was unbearably painful and it didn't help that when we entered the building there were kids screaming and crying while receiving the shot and kids trying to escape from the line before getting to the shot. Occasionally one would get away and the chase would be on. It was the only thing fun about the whole ordeal! Moms trying to keep hold of their own child(ren) while scurrying about trying to help the mother corner the runaway before they could find an exit. When finally cornered the poor thing would be grabbed by an appendage (usually an arm, but not always) and usually a him (but not always) and drug back in line. Quite entertaining actually and I don't recall any of them successfully avoiding the painful process anyway. I don't know if the tick shot was effective or if we were never exposed to the Rocky Mountain tick fever but in any event, I don't think we ever contracted the disease. Of course, the way we lived it could have just gone undetected.

They brought a portable x-ray machine to each site, like the Sand Springs store or the Winnett courthouse for the annual x-ray. I don't know what the x-ray was for, they may have been searching for TB, but I don't know for sure. I'm sure we received a goodly portion of radiation back in those days for whatever the reason.

We moved back to the original homestead from there. We had very little in those days but we didn't know it so we were gleefully happy with little more than a full stomach.

The neighbors were far and few between at that time and are actually even fewer now in that area as I write this in 2022. Our closest neighbors were Grandpa and Grandma. My paternal grandfather, David, was born and reared in Kansas, migrated to Galveston, Texas, and when his meat shop flooded out during a hurricane he came to Montana and homesteaded on the highest, driest hill he could find (1885-1967). My paternal grandmother Nora Nell Hetrick Petersen (1898-1983) was born a triplet but Dora Dell and Cora Bell died as infants. They lived about two and a half miles east. The next closest were down on the Musselshell River which was five or six miles but that, however, did not deter us from visiting them frequently.

In the winter Dad would harness the team after supper and hook them to the bobsled which Mom would have prepared with heated flat irons (the irons used, with detachable handle, to iron our clothes) to help keep our feet from freezing on the way. When our faces got too cold Mom would throw a quilt over us. During those visits the folks would play cards and we and their kids would entertain ourselves usually outside even in the cold. I recall on our way home on clear nights how beautiful the stars were twinkling in the cold clear air. Occasionally Mom and Dad would sing old ballads as we traveled through the stillness with just the sound of the harnesses clanking and the horse's hooves plodding along on the frozen ground. In the summer it was the same drill only we used the wagon.

We had another neighbor by the name of Walter that was a bachelor living on a homestead several miles north of us. He didn't have a vehicle so when he needed to go to town (Jordan) he would walk to Mosby (about twelve miles) and hitch a ride with a neighbor going that way. On one particular trip he was returning from Jordan with Marcus Matovich when they met a neighbor going toward Jordan that Walter recognized and wanted to talk to so he opened the truck door and stepped out. Amazingly he tore his clothes up and drew blood from numerous locations but apparently no broken bones.

He used to walk by our house on his way home, usually in the middle of the night, and he would start hollering very loud from a quarter mile away. I'm not sure what that was about but maybe he wanted Dad to know who was going by or hoping Dad would be awakened and light the lamp so he could stop in and visit, which happened on more than one occasion.

He done all his haying, as most did, with horses and one time the horses took off unexpectedly and ran over his foot with the rake wheel. I don't know if bones were broken but it swelled so badly he couldn't get his shoe on so he was wearing an overshoe instead in the high heat of summer.

He never did get a vehicle, but his neighbor (and rival, they did not like each other for some reason) Wren Niles did get a used quarter-ton pickup but of course he didn't know how to drive. My uncle Elmer took it upon himself to teach him. I don't know whose fault it was, Elmer's or Wren's, but he never learned to drive very well. One time Wren was at Phil Matovich's place and his pickup wouldn't start. Elmer was there but he knew better than to pull him to start it so he pulled him up a hill backwards then turned him loose to roll down to get it started. He got to the bottom and no start so he pulled him up again. To the bottom without starting again so Elmer asked him what gear he was trying it in. He said he was trying it in neutral as he was taught; you always start it in neutral!

Wren was quite hard of hearing so he always had the engine running at a very high RPM when he would take off. We were at Mosby one time when Wren stopped for fuel. When ready to leave he floored the gas pedal and slipped his foot off the clutch. He spewed gravel all over the lot as the pickup jitterbugged and fishtailed toward the pavement where the hind wheels squealed a bit; then he shifted to high gear and went *kerchunk kerchunk kerchunk* and proceeded at about ten miles an hour which was his top speed.

It amazes me how times have changed from then until now. Our neighbors today live one-tenth of a mile away and we have autos with air conditioning and heaters and about the only time we visit the neighbors is when we run across them in town at the grocery store.

When Larry became school age the closest school was seventeen miles away so he had to stay with the Thomas's near Sand Springs. That was not a good year for him as he was homesick and didn't get a good start in school. The next year Donny was also going to need to go so Dad took a job running the Odie place one mile north of Sand Springs. It came equipped with a real house, barn, root cellar, electricity and other amenities not including indoor plumbing however. This move was precipitated by there being a school at Sand Springs where the boys could walk to school. I was four years old when we arrived there in the spring of 1948.

That August when school started I went out to tell my brothers goodbye as they headed out to walk the mile to the first day of school that year. The screen door slammed behind me and I found that I couldn't reach the handle to get back in the house so I followed my brothers to school.

Donny had given me my "kindergarten" (which didn't exist at that time) at home, teaching me the alphabet and how to count along with Mom helping him teach me to read so I was quite prepared for school. I got good mileage out of telling the teacher that Mom had locked me out of the house. The teacher accommodated me with first-grade materials and my brothers shared their lunch with me so I had a wonderful day. That night on the way home I got to thinking and worrying a bit about Mom and whether she might be looking for me. We had no phones of course so she had no easy way to check. My worries turned out to be unfounded however, thankfully, as she said not a word about my absence. I concluded from that, that I was such a perfect child she just hadn't missed me! Anyway the next morning there were three lunches ready so I went back to school. There were some tough trips to school that winter as there were no trees so the wind and snow were brutal at times. Brother Larry always, as the biggest and oldest I guess, broke trail with me following and Donny bringing up the rear to make sure I didn't lag behind. They took such good care of me (of course I didn't realize it at the time) but in retrospect, I am humbled by their compassion and care.

I remember one especially miserable morning with a heavy snow falling, very cold and a strong west wind, it was a full-fledged blizzard. We were so cold and visibility wasn't good so we were stopping often and huddling together to try to stay warm and on course. Suddenly Larry looked back and seen a silhouette carrying something long in hand. He concluded it was Dad with the razor strop coming to speed us up so as not to be late for school. Just as suddenly we were no longer cold and made a beeline for school. It turned out to be Mom with some extra scarves for us but she was not able to catch us. What a treasure she was, so loving and caring, sacrificing her safety for ours.

Cars and Wrecks

Sometime that winter Dad bought his first car. It was a well-used 1935 Chevy two-seater four door with a wood and tar paper roof. Wow, we were so impressed. Of course a pecking order was established right away. Donny and Larry got the back window seats and I got the middle. I remember one of the early trips we went on was to go to Grandpa and Grandma Barker's place (my birthplace except they had a new house). There was quite a little snow and we got stuck. Dad dug us out and put chains on the rear. That got us moving but there was lots of noise and chatter as we chugged along. Donny had his head out the window watching what was going on. I had no window so I was pestering him for my turn to look. He finally conceded but I wasn't to look long. I got on my knees and leaned across him to get my head out. It was fascinating watching the wheel spin and the chains digging up dirt through the snow. After what I thought was a very insignificant amount of time Donny said my turn was up. I ignored him and he told me again, and again, I ignored him so he rolled the window up on my neck. I couldn't speak, all I could do was kick so he finally rolled it down and I quickly conceded my turn was indeed up.

Grandpa Barker's house sat very close to a very sharp hill drop-off with only a driveway between the house and crest. When we were about ready to leave Larry got permission to start the car. The car had a manual transmission and Dad had parked it in reverse so it wouldn't roll. Apparently Larry didn't know all the details about clutches etc. so he started it without pushing in the clutch and it immediately backed up and over the bank. Fortunately it didn't roll over. I don't remember the rescue and retrieval project but it all worked out and I'm sure that was a big first step in Larry's driver's education program.

I remember a couple other notable times on trips with the "new" car after we had moved back to the homestead. We were on the way to Winnett (first time ever) on the paved road when the rear left corner of the car dropped drastically. Then we see the rear wheel with axle extending toward the car passing us. Dad got the car stopped and retrieved the wheel and axle that had gone down the road a significant distance before running into the opposite side ditch.

I also recall another occasion in the "new" car. We were returning at night from visiting Bob and Flossie (Dad's sister) Eike at Cat Creek coming down Cat Creek hill which had a sharp right-hand turn at the bottom to line up with a very narrow wooden bridge when the lights went out. I can hear Mom yet today as she screamed in fright. The old mechanical brakes made sudden stops a non-option so I have no idea how Dad managed to hit the bridge in the middle and get stopped at the foot of the hill going out the other side, but he did. Although I didn't know much about God then, I know now that he has been watching over us for a long time.

Devastating Dismissal

Late that winter, I remember well, it was Valentine's Day week, the county superintendent of schools, Mrs. Pollard, came by for an inspection and found me. She declared that I was too young to be in first grade so she ordered me not to return. I was devastated but respected authority so I hung around until school adjourned for the day and went home with my brothers. To my disappointment my mom wasn't too upset and basically told me to get over it.

That spring us "young adults" as we thought of ourselves were out exploring around a large reservoir a short distance from home when one of us discovered a nest of duck eggs with no duck around. In retrospect we undoubtedly flushed her off but they looked abandoned to us so we took them home. Mom had a hen setting so we slipped them in amongst her eggs while she was off feeding. The setting hen did not reject them and dutifully sat on them until they hatched. Shortly thereafter the fun started.

Mom was a bit surprised to see the hen had hatched some ducklings but not nearly as surprised as the hen. The ducklings were still very tiny when they found the nearby "crick." They took to it like ducks to water! The hen however did not, so she would run back and forth along the shore clucking and clucking to them until they came back and she would herd them back to the nest and try to dry them off. We now know how cruel and frustrating that was to the mother hen but at that time it was great entertainment for us as we didn't have a lot of entertainment options.

Another incident that still impacts me today was an excursion we all three were on along the county road that went north on the east side of the mentioned creek (better known as the crick). We flushed a rabbit and he ran into a small culvert under the road. I, being the smallest, was elected to go in and flush it out the other end where he would be caught by Larry and Donny. It was chilly that day so I had on a coat which I did not remove before forcing my way into the culvert. It was an extremely tight fit and after my feet were about three feet inside I encountered a buildup of silt on the bottom of the culvert making it too tight to proceed. I then began to wiggle backwards to escape. It was a corrugated culvert so in the tightness my coat bunched up right away and I was solidly wedged and I couldn't go either way. Unbeknownst to me the rabbit had escaped unscathed from the other end so my brothers were wandering on down the road looking for the next entertainment opportunity. I was finding it very difficult to breathe but I don't know if that was from the tight quarters or just sheer panic. I was screaming for help when I did have enough breath and Donny finally heard me, so each of them was able to get a hold of a foot and forcefully remove me. I have been claustrophobic ever since that day. Even now when I get into an elevator I have to concentrate on what I will be doing when I get out to keep myself calm in that tight space. I do like the glass elevators where I can see out but they are scarce.

Another memory from that time was when the crick was running very high in the spring. We needed to get across but I don't remember why. It must have been important though as Dad saddled a horse and he put us, one at a time, up on the neck of the horse in front of the saddle where he could hold on to us, then he laid face down across the saddle with his feet out over the rump and swam the horse across. After unloading each one he would swim the horse back across to get the next one.

One other recollectable memory was a dead cow carcass we discovered way out by a field north of the house. It probably died while calving or who knows what but it had been there for a long time. It stunk quite strongly but the hide and skeleton were pretty much petrified. It was completely hollowed out so we began to explore inside. It was a little cooler in there but the smell was staggering.

Then we spotted the snakes—oooohwee—yikes!! There was only one entrance in the rear going in but there was two exits coming out. We did more damage to that carcass in two seconds than the weather had done in a year or so!

I think it was somewhere around this time that Dad took us to the zoo. We really didn't care for it that much so within about a week we escaped and found our way home!

POINTS TO PONDER

Must you sit down before you can sit up?

CHAPTER 2
MOVING ON

WHEN SCHOOL WAS out that spring my folks moved again. Late that summer before school started I got lucky and found where they had moved to.

It was back to the homestead which was a small dry land ranch, dry and small being the key words here. I never did meet Ace Reid but he obviously stayed with us a lot during those years to have been able to write the documentaries of our family life so accurately that he put on calendars and in books and magazines.

Following is a list of some of the things we didn't have that will give you a better understanding of what not having much meant:

- No running water
- No indoor bathroom
- No garbage barrel. Let that sink in a second, we had no garbage. Anything combustible went in the stoves; flour and sugar came in cloth sacks with print designs so Mom made clothes and towels from them. No cans, everything was canned in glass; she reused the jars and the rings and the lids were used to cover knot holes in the granary or toys. Any spoiled leftovers and other edible type waste went in the slop bucket and fed to the butcher hogs.

- No refrigerator
- No thermostat
- No electricity
- No phone
- No road
- No TV
- No toilet paper
- No mailbox or mailman
- No school bus
- I could go on but hopefully you get the picture.

However we did have a lot of things as well. Like we always had *enough* to eat; I know this, as the old saying goes, because anytime I asked for more Mom would say, "You've had *enough.*" I'm just kidding as we may not have had much selection but we always had all we wanted to eat. The folks worked outside jobs for neighbors frequently and wouldn't be home sometimes when we got home from school so I got (or had) to learn how to cook (my brothers would dispute that statement), nothing fancy, just the staples we had on hand.

Here is a partial list of things we did have:

- We had a bobsled.
- We had a team.
- We had a wagon.
- We had saddle horses.
- We had a milk cow.
- We had an outhouse with Sears and Roebuck and Montgomery Ward catalogues (boy those soft index pages went fast).

- We had a churn and Mom invented another one of those. She would fill a gallon jar ¾ full of cream, put it halfway down a gunny sack and tie the ends on each side behind her saddle and ride the five miles to Mosby to get the mail and when she got back she had butter and buttermilk in the gallon jar.

- We had hogs for reproduction and meat.

- We had chickens both for eggs and eating.

- We also had a screen door. It was to keep the flies IN (it was very effective).

- We had a wood burning cookstove in the kitchen which heated that area both summer (especially summer) and winter and a heating stove in the bedroom for winter warmth. The bedroom had two beds—one for the folks and one for us three boys— two with heads on one end and one with a head on the other, which meant six feet in the middle, which led to some pretty good kicking matches and someone (not me of course) seemed too often to have cold feet which was another distraction.

- We had a separator – Now most of you probably know what those are but for you youngsters who don't, the separator was a piece of cloth about the size of a dishtowel. You folded it over like a bandana (that was so the holes didn't match) then you held it over the edge of the milk bucket and poured the milk through it, thus separating most of the hair and larger chunks from the milk.

- We also had a flower planter. You've all seen them, the ones with the four black legs and the large stainless steel flowerpot and the long handle on one side to hang a flower basket on. Well my folks didn't get out much so they didn't know what it was, so they would dump milk in the big stainless steel flowerpot and make us kids turn the handle so the milk and cream came out the drain tubes in front. Fortunately it took too much water to clean it up so they didn't use it often.

- We had an icebox as well which served several purposes. It provided us another chore in the morning going to the icehouse chipping off ice and filling the ice tray on top. We then had the evening chore of taking the melted ice water out to water the garden. And last but not least it kept the milk at room temperature 24-7. If you forgot and left the milk out at night it would take on a bit of a chill but in the "icebox" it was at constant room temperature, very effective it was. Also whenever we had a thunderstorm with lots of lightning in the evening all the milk would be sour the next morning. I never did pursue the explanation for that but it happened every time.

- And speaking of thunderstorms I recall one late afternoon the sky turned black and threatening looking and Dad was out with the team. He came in with the team running. He got them unhooked from the wagon but didn't have time to put them in the barn so he tied them to the corral fence and came running to the house. It was a very violent storm and obviously had a twister in it. It picked the hayrack off of its running gear and twirled it around a few times and set it down gently in the hog pen without damage, unreal!

- So as you can see we had everything we needed and we didn't know we were poor, so we were blissfully happy.

I mentioned the icehouse and being on a small dry farm might take some explanation. The icehouse was dug into the side of the slope just east of the house with logs for sides and logs for a roof that was then covered with dirt. In the winter we would take the bobsled in tow with the team to the neighbors on the Musselshell River. Dad would chop a hole in the ice about a foot thick big enough to get the crosscut saw through. He would then saw out squares of ice which would float and he had ice tongs to get hold of them and lift them out and load the sled. We would carry these into the "root cellar" type icehouse, stack them together and cover them with sawdust. We then had ice all summer and until the river froze over good the next year, then repeat the process.

The move back to the homestead was precipitated by Dad and others getting a school up and going just three miles south of home. This meant I was going to be able to go to a different school, which I did. We had a very small sort of a tar paper one classroom schoolhouse (shack) with small enclosed porch to leave overshoes and coats in on the days we didn't need them in the classroom. We had a young lady in her first year of teaching by the name of Ms. Fox and she had seven different grades to teach in the one room. She lived in Winnett and commuted daily the twenty-two highway miles and two dirt "road" miles as there was nowhere to live nearby.

I was her only first grader and she had one second grader. I had basically had first grade last year so I was a bit of a problem for her as she couldn't keep me busy. By Christmastime I had completed all the first-grade workbooks and materials she had so when we came back after Christmas she put me in second grade with Donna Mosby. I successfully completed second grade the last half of that school term so I started third grade that fall at age six.

That three-mile hike still holds many good and bad memories for me. All but one-half mile of this route was somewhat protected from the wind with scattered trees but I remember that half mile well when it was fourteen below zero with an east wind. Once again Larry broke trail and Donny and I huddled as close to him as possible for some protection from the elements. When we finally got to school we were surprised that no one else was there. Larry built a fire in the wood stove and we huddled around it until about nine o'clock and no one came so we let the fire burn down and left for the long trek back. That was the only time I remember that happening.

But when the weather was nice we made the trips kinda fun as amongst other side ventures we developed three shortcuts on the route. As I said it was three miles by the "road," but if you took all three shortcuts on the same trip it was only four miles.

We had to cross a road that went to some oil wells down toward the Musselshell River. A gentleman by the name of Tony Garcia took care of those wells. He and his family lived in Lewistown and Tony commuted the seventy-seven miles to Mosby by car every day. He parked his car there and took his jeep pickup on the dirt roads to the wells. On rare occasions we would hear him coming out in the PM and be close enough that we could rush to be crossing the road when he got there. We loved these encounters as he was very friendly and would stop and chat a moment. He had a Spanish accent that we had never heard before and we loved it. He also smoked cigars and the faint smell of the smoke also was enjoyed. I recall only once that on a particularly windy wet cold afternoon he loaded us up and took us the last mile and a half home. That was really a highlight for us.

We also had other adventures on those trips. I recall once when we stumbled upon a crippled meadowlark. She flushed out from under a sagebrush with a crippled wing dragging on one side. We decided we better catch her and render first aid. We could get within about three or four feet and she would flutter off another ten feet and commence hobbling along with the wing dragging. This went on for about a quarter mile and we could get so close but couldn't quite catch her and she finally flew off and made a big circle and landed where we first flushed her. Another of those teachable moments, she couldn't be gone from her nest too long!

On another occasion we found a snake not far from a huge red anthill. We whacked it a few times with sagebrush stalks and had it pretty dizzy, then we carried it to the anthill and stirred the hill up with the stalks getting the ants furious then we put the snake on the tore up anthill. They attacked with vengeance but we couldn't stay for the rest of the show without being late for school. We checked the ant's progress twice a day and within a week there was only a bare skeleton of clean white bones left of the snake. It was quite impressive as we didn't realize snakes had ribs and a backbone. It was quite delicate but we managed to get it to school in pretty good shape so the teacher and our classmates could enjoy and learn from our experiment. We thought it worthy of decorating the teacher's desk but she thought otherwise so out it went!

Tragedy and Trauma Strike

The fall of 1950 brought tragedy to our family. Uncle Dan Petersen and wife Edna were hunting deer north of where we lived and he killed a large mule deer that he couldn't get out by himself. They came to our place for help. Edna stayed there and Dad and Larry went with Dan to get the deer. Dan was driving his old army jeep with a full metal cab and they were traversing the top of a narrow ridge attempting to go up a very steep grade. The jeep powered out and the brakes wouldn't hold it so they were descending backward down the grade.

Dan opened his door to see back in an attempt to keep it on top the ridge. Dad put his feet and head out his narrow window and exited just as they sideswiped a small pine tree on Dad's side, breaking an ankle in the process. The tree caused the jeep to roll over on Dan's side. When it rolled it was going over the side of the ridge so it rolled over and over numerous times until reaching the bottom. With his door open Dan was ejected and squashed by the tumbling jeep. Larry was inside in the back of the cab so he rode all the way to the bottom tumbling with axes, jacks, tools, etc. When it finally stopped rolling over at the bottom he crawled out bleeding badly from gashes on the back of his head. Dad had crawled down to Dan and was holding his head but he was already deceased.

Dad told Larry to head for home and get help. I don't know how many miles that would have been but I'm sure it was more than two. Larry was holding his hands to the back of his head as he walked and ran to try to stem the blood flow. He told me later he wanted to lie down and take a nap but then he would think of Dad and Dan and force himself on. Fortunately he was seen by Uncle Carroll Hough who was out hunting on horseback. He was able to get Larry on the back of his saddle and brought him on home. Carroll and others went back in his car and retrieved Dan's body and Dad. They stopped at the house and I remember looking through the window into the back seat where Dan's body was covered with a blanket. This was very traumatic for a six-year-old who hadn't experienced human death before.

Carroll then left with Larry, Dad, and the body for Lewistown. Dad was admitted to the hospital as the swelling was so bad they couldn't cast it until they got the swelling down the next morning. That was the only hospital stay he would have in his 90-plus years of life. Dan left behind his widow Edna and their three young sons Daniel, Arthur, and William.

Dad was on crutches for what seemed like forever at the time but was probably only about six weeks. He got extremely good on the crutches as he still had to do the chores and many other tasks just to survive. I recall one night we were returning from Grandpa Petersen's with the old pickup Dad had acquired. It had rained and snowed so it was very slick and we slid into a washout and was stuck. We had to walk the mile home in the mud with Dad on his crutches. We had never been able to outrun Dad so we thought, now is our opportunity. We taunted him a little then took off running. We didn't get far before he passed us on his crutches. Amazing and humiliating so we didn't try that again!

POINTS TO PONDER

Why does the house always burn down
but the contents burn up?

CHAPTER 3
MEMORIES OF THE HOMESTEAD

Hauling Water

In those years we had to haul our house and drinking water about a half mile from a hand dug well. We had a pump but the leathers were usually not good enough to get the thing primed so we mostly dipped it with a bucket and rope and put it in wooden barrels on either the wagon or the bobsled depending on conditions. There was a short but very steep incline getting out of the coulee where the well was located. I remember on one occasion it was very cold, I believe about ten below, after having had some sunny days that created a lot of icy conditions. We had the barrels full and Dad headed the team up the steep grade pulling the bobsled. The ground was so slick with frost that the team couldn't hold on. As they fell the weight of the sled pulled them back down the slope with the sled jackknifing enough to tip the barrels over—so now we had added a significant amount of ice to the mess and we were again out of water. After refilling the barrels Dad made a significant detour down the coulee to a different draw that we were able to get out on.

Speaking of water barrels, Mom had a serious injury while attempting to move a half full barrel by tipping it and rolling it on the bottom edge. The water sloshed and overpowered her, coming down on her ankle, cutting it severely. I don't remember whether we were at home or at Dad's folks' place and I don't remember who, but someone, probably Dad, got her to the doctor for repairs. She had a very painful but fortunately full recovery, but carried serious scars thereafter.

The water barrels were made of wooden stays held together with metal bands. If they weren't used regularly they would dry out, shrink, and leak until soaked up again. We boys didn't understand all this technology so one winter we discovered a barrel that had loose stays. This to us meant that logically it would not hold water so it was useless as a barrel. We dismantled it and were making snow skis out of the stays. Sometime prior to our first slalom attempt Dad found us and needless to say he was not a happy camper. I can tell you it is much, much simpler to dismantle a wooden barrel than to reconstruct one. We tried and tried but I don't believe that barrel ever held water again. Looking back I am a little surprised that we didn't have to hand carry water from the well the half mile to the house to make up for the missing barrel.

Bum Lambs

One of the outside jobs that Dad took every year in the spring was lambing. He lambed for several different owners but in particular it was Joe Dutton and Lou Hill. He would be gone for about a month at a time but since we had an old pickup by then we would get to go see him occasionally. He would send bum lambs home with us to raise. We bottle fed them with skimmed milk so they didn't thrive well and tended to have extended stomachs. The only time they got whole milk was when both Mom and Dad were gone. That saved separating (remember the separator) and skimming the cream and the clean up and the lambs loved it, it was a win-win for all. Mom did ask occasionally where the cream was and of course it had accidently gotten spilt. I doubt she bought that but she didn't persist, whew! I'm not sure where Dad sold them for us in the fall but he did and we got the money.

My New 22 Rifle

I'm not sure but I believe it was the fall of 1954 that we had a good number of bums survive and sold. This resulted in me having enough money to order a 22 rifle from the Sears and Roebuck catalogue for $24.95. The two weeks it took to arrive seemed like a lifetime as I bugged Mom every day to go for the mail. Well everyday did not happen but once a week did and the second week I unwrapped this beautiful shiny JC Higgins rifle. The downside was that it required ammunition to be of much value and that cost money and was not readily available to us out in the wilderness. I was able to get some though and that winter Dad would take me spotlight hunting for jackrabbits. They would freeze and keep until the folks would go to town where they were sold for the fur and fox farm feed. This cycle led to more ammo, yea! A couple years later I was able to acquire a 4-power weaver scope for it that helped my marksmanship considerably, making the ammo go further.

My Dislike of Magpies

My dislike for magpies began in the pigpen. We would carry the slop bucket down there and dump it in a wooden trough for the hogs to feed on. The magpies would be waiting for the feeding and compete with the hogs for the food. The hogs got to the point they wouldn't even try to snap at them as they would just flutter a foot or two and return.

On a warm and sunny day one summer I was riding horseback with Dad and we came upon one of his replacement yearling heifers bogged in mud trying to get to water in a reservoir. She was alive but the magpies had pecked a hole in her upper side and were eating her guts out. Dad got her pulled out of the bog but she died anyway. This further galvanized my dislike for magpies that lasts to this day. We could at that time get five cents for a pair of magpie legs and a penny a piece for eggs. I became a very willing participant in this bounty program. My 22 rifle would net me a few cents on each magpie if I didn't miss and take more than one shell. I know now they do some good, cleaning up roadkill, etc., but it doesn't, in my mind, make up for the bad including the 4:00 AM wake up calls in the spring when they are trying to teach their young ones how to be as loud and obnoxious as the adults.

New Schoolhouse

Dad and others moved another much larger building in from somewhere. It was set up as the schoolhouse so the old one could be used as a residence for the teacher (teacherage) as there was nowhere near to house them. We had seven different teachers in the seven years I was there. They were Alice Fox 49/50, Jeannette Thomas 50/51, Katherine Stoup 51/52, Glenda (Gunda) Shaw 52/53, Jacqueline Gilfeather 53/54, Delores Hill 54/55, and Winona Nordahl 55/56. This made it quite obvious that we were pretty good educators ourselves as the teachers learned all they needed to know in one year, a feat we were quite pleased with.

We didn't have many toys to play with, but we did have a ball to play Anti-I-Over the schoolhouse. Actually it started out as a jagged rock but by the time all the shingles were gone off the roof of the new schoolhouse it was pretty well rounded out like a ball. No one ever denied it when they were tagged. All you had to do was hold the "ball" out behind their elbow so when it came back as they were running they would let everyone know they had been tagged!

School Protocol

At the start of each school year we always got there early so we could pick our own desk and placement before the new teacher arrived. Brother Larry always started out in the back row but always within a couple weeks he would be reassigned to the front row right in front of the teacher's desk. I remember one time after his reassignment we were acting up in some manner and became what the teacher would mistakenly describe as uncontrollable. She turned to the blackboard and started writing in the upper left-hand corner repeatedly "I shalt not kill." It looked like she might be there quite awhile so Larry turned his desk around facing us and began entertaining us. The teacher (referred to by us as the warden because we were incarcerated in the schoolhouse most of the time) turned and seen him and grabbed her yardstick. That was the first I realized Larry had eyes in the back of his head as he ducked just as she brought the ruler down and it snapped in two over the line of books across the front of her desk. She became a little hysterical and irrational and said there would be no more recesses (parole) for a week. A little harsh, wouldn't you think? That threat lasted until the following afternoon when she suddenly announced recess time, saying something about needing some relief. I guess she could see we were getting a little tense and pretty stressed out and needed a break.

The school was equipped with a gold colored hand bell. When we would get paroled at recess time and the weather was nice we would go down amongst the cedar trees and catch scorpions and aggravate them into fighting one another. When it was time for us to be re-incarcerated the warden would come out on the step and ring the bell. That worked pretty well when the clapper wasn't missing. One day after lunch we were down in the trees for awhile and suddenly I heard the warden screaming and hollering. I told Larry it sounded like she may have broken a leg or something bad. He said no, she was actually saying we could go fishing, so we headed for the river which was only two or three miles west. On the way Larry showed me this beautiful gold colored set line sinker. It was a little round ball with a stem on it with a sort of hook on the end to tie the line on. We didn't catch any fish but we had a lot of fun trying and there were a lot more rocks in the river when we left than when we got there.

When the weather was bad and we didn't want to go outside for our fifteen-minute parole we would play games inside. Those sessions seldom ended well as we had to have our physical activity whether outside or in. We had one old windup clock that set on the windowsill by the pencil sharpener (no wrist watches or pocket watches or cell phones in those days in our area anyway) so the old clock was gospel. It had been knocked off so many times during our "games" that the face was missing, exposing the hands so they had been straightened many times but it still worked.

Starting sometime in the spring on real nice days shortly after the afternoon parole, Larry's pencil would need sharpening and very quickly it would be time for school to adjourn. This was well received by all the students but the teacher seemed to be perplexed as to why she couldn't seem to get through all the material of the last period of the day. After several of these events on Friday afternoons the teacher's pencil would need sharpening in early afternoon and shortly thereafter it was time to adjourn. The only downside of this was occasionally adjournment time came early enough that we missed our PM parole!

The Bicycle Wreck(s)

Donny had acquired an old bike somehow. It was not a bicycle with all the amenities like we seen in the catalogue. It had no fenders, no basket, no rubber grips on the handle bars, no padding on the seat, just a bare metal plate held together by rust, no lights, no reflectors, no foot pedals, just little round steel shafts sticking out and one of them was bent so his foot would slip off sometimes on a heavy pull (which made the steel seat *very* uncomfortable but he was able to father children later on so no permanent damage), no brakes (Donny used his feet to stop it. I say feet instead of shoes because the soles were gone off his shoes so he did stop it with his feet), or chain guard so the right leg of Donny's pants were chewed off up to about mid-calf level like the rats had gotten to them and the worst part of that was them would be my new pants next year.

One time he was cruising toward home coming out of the lane when the chain again grabbed his pant leg and that dislodged it from the sprocket. He was attempting to get the chain back on and was leaning over totally distracted so he veered off the road and headed for the pond. He arrived at the pond going full speed and made quite a "splash." I helped him drag it out and he slipped the chain back on and rode it to the house to get his dry set of clothes.

I have another memory of a trip to school when I was probably about seven or eight years old. We had one hill that stood out from all the rest that we affectionately called the "big hill." Donny was riding his "bike" and he waited at the top and when I finally got there he offered me a ride down the other side. Needless to say I promptly accepted so he helped me up on the handlebars. He gave me two orders: "Don't stick your foot in the spokes behind the fork over the front wheel" and "Hang on." He knew me well enough to know he must explain why so I wouldn't have to find out on my own. He said if I got my foot in the spokes behind the fork, as it was cutting my foot off, it would damage the spokes and he had no extras, and he said if I didn't hang on I would fall off and he would run over me and that could lead to an accident which might cause injury to the bike.

With that we were off with Donny peddling as hard as he could. Soon enough gravity kicked in and he couldn't keep up so then we were on cruise—no control, just cruise.

Well the last half of the hill was a precipice similar to an Alpine ski run. We topped that at what I thought was full speed. I was wrong, as our further acceleration was instant and dramatic. At the foot of the hill there was a fork in the road—well it wasn't actually a fork and it wasn't actually a road either, it was just two wagon tracks with the sagebrush wore off and the fork was more of a right-hand approach. I was obviously the leader of this expedition and I was eyeballing the straightaway where we could wind down, sorta like the runaway truck ramps you see nowadays.

The problem was Donny was the head of operations and he was a little stubborn—oh, sorry Donny—he was kind of a determined young man and our destination called for us to make the turn.

He banked the bike so far to the right that I thought we were going to crash to the right so I was leaning left as far as I could which probably wasn't helping him much, visibility maybe! Well, there was no tread on the sidewall of the tires; of course there wasn't any on the face of them either, so the bike skidded into a rut. That's when

I figured out that this was a physics lesson as from this angle and speed it set the trajectory and velocity of our launch such that our flight path would carry us beyond the reach of the shrapnel that was soon to follow, and it worked.

During Donny's dismount, as hasty as it was, he had managed to damage his (my) pants by tearing the entire inseam out on the right leg and I had managed to ruin my underwear by…never mind. I tell you this because in those days we had very little so this was serious. You see the clothes we had on were the better half of our entire wardrobes. So this meant that the pair of clothes back home was now the better half—again. You see we really didn't ruin anything back then we just degraded them.

Then I noticed Donny had also removed the hide off both his elbows and replaced it with dirt. From previous experiences we knew not to try scraping it off for a couple reasons. One, it hurt to scrape on a fresh wound, and two—and more importantly—the dirt was a very effective clotting agent so you didn't have to hold your elbows out so long to keep the blood off your clothes.

I didn't get to see much of the wreck as most of it occurred behind me, but judging by the size of the debris field and the location of the bicycle carcass and Donny's incessant attention to detail it had to be at least a nine, maybe better!

Many Inventions

By not having much it brought out the ingenuity in us and we invented many things. The folks did have a static machine. It was neat. It stood on the floor and was housed in a wooden box about two feet tall. It had neat scroll holes cut near the top with cloth covers on them and that's where the static came out. It worked on a battery so we kids were not to touch it (unless the folks were gone, "ahem"). It had a wing nut on the back (which alone debunked my brother's claim that I was the only wing nut on the place) with a wire attached that ran out through the crack by the kitchen window and attached on the outside to the clothes line.

I figured out that this was a lightning detector. They would have a perfectly clear static going on and a thunderstorm would roll by the coast of Guam or somewhere and it would suddenly detect it and go KACHEEshshshshsh. It had a tuner knob and a volume knob. The tuner would change the pitch of the static from mushy to shrill (like a siren) to running water sound. Mom was always in charge of selecting the static they were to listen to. They would then pull their kitchen chairs over in front of it, sit down and lean over and cup their ear with their hand so they wouldn't miss any of the static. Mom would turn it down a little to save on the battery. This was a Saturday night ritual.

Dad apparently didn't have the tolerance for pain that Mom did so he invented aerobics. He would get up and walk around rotating his head on his stiff neck and swing his cup arm around and around. He would then sit back down and ask Mom what he had missed. She was very good to him and would repeat everything that went on while he was gone--"SHSHSHSHSHSHSHSHSH."

This inspired me to see if I could replicate this static machine without the battery. Dad had brought home an old tire from the Mosby service station that he used between the team and the "new" car when it was stuck in the mud or snow. It softened the blow when the team hit the end of the chain to avoid pulling the bumper off (again). I put some rocks and dirt inside the tire and rolled it. SHSHSHSH, it sounded just like the static machine. I showed it to my brothers and of course they were impressed. It was jointly decided we should roll it to the top of the hill behind the house and see if it could work on perpetual motion.

Speaking of the little hill, it proved my brother wrong showing the world wasn't flat. From the top of the hill you could also see that the warden's theory was wrong as well. Her theory was that the world was round like a ball but from the top of the hill you could see the edges of the world all the way around so it was obvious that the world was round alright but like a doily not a ball.

Anyway we got the static machine up there and lined it up to go between the house and the chicken coop with the pond beyond the target destination and with a push, set it in motion. It worked well for a short way but it picked up speed quickly and the rocks quit sliding around inside which threw it out of balance. It began taking big steps instead of rolling smoothly and they got bigger and bigger. As it stepped higher and higher it began to veer off course. It took aim at the chicken coup which had a high chicken wire fence around it. It connected at about the five foot level. At that moment Mom had stepped out of the house and seen it. The fence screeched at the same time as Mom so we had invented stereo, if only for a moment.

Well Mom, not to be outdone, invented the power walk straight toward us. Having never seen the power walk before we didn't know what it was and it was looking a bit threatening so we quickly took off down the lane as our escape route. The lane consisted of a barbed wire fence on each side and a barbed wire gate across the end around the corner out of sight.

My brothers were much faster than I was so they were out of sight when I reached the gate. Well, I looked back and Mom was really outdoing herself today as she was now inventing the relay race. She had a baton about three feet long made out of an inch and a half pipe and she was coming on strong (they have since modified the baton to a small piece of plastic). Of course I had never seen the relay before either so it also looked quite threatening. So for self-preservation I had to invent another technique of my own. I dropped to the ground and rolled under the gate, sprang up on the other side, and accelerated again.

That move was adopted worldwide in later years known as the "stop, drop, and roll," but of course I got no credit for it. Mom witnessed this successful maneuver and tried to replicate it. Unfortunately for her she was a bit thicker than I so as she rolled under the gate the bottom barbed wire snagged her dress on the hip and pulled her dress a little askew then snapped into place down her backside, pinning her face down under the gate. She began shouting somewhat hysterically. I stopped and cautiously made my way back thinking it could be a trap. The baton had rolled on through the gate so I kicked it gently to make sure it was out of her reach.

She was lying perfectly still so I cautiously worked my way back and she requested that I gently open the blankety-blank gate. I had never heard her refer to the gate in those terms before so I assumed this must be a serious matter. The gate was too tight for me to open but not to worry, I had seen Dad solve this problem with tight gates before. He would place his foot on the bottom wire and both hands on the top wire and reef back and forth until he gained enough slack to open it easily and gently.

So, I gently placed my hands on the top wire and my foot on the bottom wire. Then I clomped down sharply—when I did this my other foot came off the ground and I began to yo-yo back and forth from top to bottom. Somehow my efforts seemed to be exacerbating the problem and I was afraid I might be suffering permanent hearing loss from the screeching, and I don't think it was the gate doing the screeching so I turned loose and stepped back. After further analyzing the situation I concluded that the chances of her predicament being fatal was not nearly as likely as mine would be if she were to get loose, so I told her I would run and get Dad.

So I sauntered off up the lane. I soon got bored so I began counting the barbs on the wire between posts. Turns out there were an average of fifty-one, in case you're ever asked. This made me sleepy but I hated naps so I kept going. I then picked a bouquet of wild onions that were blooming nearby. My brothers were already back and were working on building some kind of snow machine so I stopped to lend them some of my engineering skills. After some time Dad must have got the chicken fence fixed as he came by and inquired whether anyone knew of Mom's whereabouts. "Oh," I said, "I have been looking all over for you." I then described to him her location and plight so he wandered off down the lane (Dad was very hard to excite).

We were working right beside the road (tracks) that Mom would be coming back on so I got to thinking I maybe shouldn't be right there. I decided to take a mini vacation. We had a hideout on the back side of the hill behind the house that we all frequently felt a need to occupy with these mini vacations to avoid prosecution in most cases. It was a washout in sandy ground so we had expanded it into sort of a cave with big spoons (not the "good spoons" Mom kept asking us if we had but old spoons we'd had for awhile). The key here was you had to stay until Mom started looking for you, however long that took.

Now my mom wasn't exactly the sharpest tack in the box as there were tens of sections of wilderness behind that little hill with untold varmints and monsters and even a river that we could drown in but do you think she ever looked there? *Nope.* She would simply walk up to the top of the hill and holler up toward that little secret washout, "It's time to come in now!"

So, there was the long-awaited welcome signal, but you had to play this part right. To avoid exposing the hideout location or letting her know you heard her you had to sit quiet for another two hours—or two seconds depending on how dark it was getting! The next key was not to pass her on the way to the house. I quietly sneaked in and went to bed.

Mom was aging by then and her memory was slipping (I think she was thirty-three at that time) but anyway she came by sometime later and I pretended to be asleep. She obviously had forgotten that she was mad at me so she leaned over and kissed me on the forehead and tucked the covers in around me. Wow, I wanted to reach up and hug her so bad but didn't think I dared, either that or I was too ashamed at that point, I don't know which. I left home not so long after that for high school and never spent much time with her again. She passed away not so many years later so don't think tucking a child in is not worth it because it doesn't last long. Please think again, and don't pass up the opportunity to do so with a child, grandchild, as the tuck I got that night from Mom has lasted me seventy years and counting and it feels as good today as it did then.

POINTS TO PONDER

Must you shut down before you can shut up?

CHAPTER 4

TEACHABLE MOMENTS

Horse Wreck

I had part-time work from time to time for neighbors riding horseback checking and/or gathering cattle and haying. On one of those occasions I was riding a mare named Sox down to Kimble's on the river to help Max ride. I took a shortcut across the "big hill" on the way and when Sox headed over the back slope of an old seismograph road she stumbled and fell, rolling over headfirst. I had not the experience nor intelligence to jump clear so she rolled right over me. I remember the saddle horn on my right side and the cantle on the left and I could see her hind legs kicking above me as she struggled to get up so I actually wasn't hurt from the rollover. It was when she got to her feet, she stepped on my right leg calf with one hind foot as she bolted away.

I began crawling for home on the trails (roads) to avoid cactus. I hadn't crawled more than a half mile when the Charles Allen family came up behind me in their car. There was almost never a car on that road so it must have been divine intervention. They took me on home and the folks got me to Jordan the next day to see Dr. Ferrand (he was also the dentist and veterinarian). He said the bone was bent but not broken so home we went. My leg was badly swollen and dark purple from the knee down. After several days I was able to get back on the horse so I went down to help ride again. I don't remember how many days we rode but I do remember trying with help to get my boot off when we got in. Sometimes I had to elevate the leg for some time before we could get the boot off.

Everything was horses and manual labor then, so haying was challenging for a youngster in those days (at least this one). I didn't mind running the horse to throw the hay up on the stack with the overshot stacker. I did not like being on the stack with the pitchfork trying to keep the sides straight up. I remember one time on the stack at the Bob Moss place when a rattlesnake came up with a load of hay. I couldn't see him but I could hear him. I'm sure I levitated two feet above the stack but Dad was there as well and he said, "Don't worry, they always go down!" (As I mentioned earlier, he was hard to excite.)

There were many horse wrecks during those years and one that really stands out for me did get Dad excited. Dad would load the bobsled with loose hay from the stack with a pitchfork and the team would pull the sled out to where the cattle were and Dad would pitch the hay off as they plodded along. We had a dog named Pal and he liked to follow along until calving season came, then Dad would make him "stay" at home.

Well one morning during calving season when we (Donny, me, and Dad) got to the cattle, unbeknown to us, Pal showed up. The cattle kinda went nuts with one cow in particular taking in after Pal, so he made a beeline to the sled and ducked in behind the team and under the sled. Well the cow came in right behind him and the wreck was on. The team took off and the box came off the running gear of the sled landing on the dog, which started howling and screaming underneath. Dad left on the running gear trying to stop the team and cussing the dog. (This time I think he was excited!) This left me and

Donny sitting on this little pile of hay with angry and hungry cows attacking the hay and still trying to get to the dog. There was cattle all the way around the sled and they were ramming each other trying to get to the hay so you can imagine how "secure" we felt with them eating the hay right out from under us and blowing snot on us.

The team finally came to a tree and one went on each side at full speed so the runaway stopped there but with considerable damage to the harness. We escaped with no physical damage but very mentally shaken and Pal survived with no noticeable physical or deleterious effects.

Brother Donny

A few other memories of my brother Donny as we grew up was his trapeze show. Our dad had built a log dugout shop in the hillside south and west of the house and Donny had tied a rope to one of the log rafters and ran it through a short piece of pipe and tied the other end to the rafter creating a high-rise swing. He would get up on the workbench and leap out and catch the pipe and swing back and forth. Dad had hand mixed concrete and done about half the floor from the workbench outward. When Donny had swung up enough momentum he would release and land on his feet just past the concrete. Well, eventually Dad had accumulated enough ingredients to concrete the rest of the floor. We kids were helping, shoveling, gravel, adding cement, mixing, shoveling the mud out, and leveling it out without trowels, so much of it done with hands. Donny took a little break, crawled up on the workbench, and announced we should watch the man on the flying trapeze and he jumped. He caught the pipe okay but when he hit the end of the first swing his wet hands lost their grip and he came down on the old concrete flat on his back.

We were startled to say the least but before we could react he was up. He rubbed the back of his head vigorously and went back to work!

On another occasion Donny and I were following Dad on foot as he headed up to the field to feed hay to the cattle carrying his pitchfork in his right hand with the tongs pointed forward. There was quite a little snow and Dad was breaking a track but he took awfully long steps. Donny was next in line and he was looking down concentrating on stepping far enough to land in Dad's footprints. He got too close and as the handle of the fork swung back as it did every step it caught Donny directly in the eye. Dad sent us back home but the damage was done. His eye swelled shut and turned a beautiful black/dark purple. I would term it a class A shiner but fortunately it had no long-lasting ill effects.

Another Teachable Moment (That Lasted Weeks)

Our dad was helping Warren Rowton with his haying operation one nice summer day and Donny and I had accompanied him. He was mowing with a little tractor with a three-point hitch mower and we were running along behind. Suddenly a large beautiful white and black animal ran out and had about six of the cutest little ones chasing after, they were so cute and shiny. Donny wanted one so he took in after them and I was close behind as I thought I needed a cute pet as well. They outran us out of the field but just as the big one was headed into a hollow log Donny got her by the tail with me right over his shoulder.

She unloaded right in our faces. Instantly I could neither see nor breathe. I really thought I was dying as I collapsed and lost consciousness. I don't know how long I was out but I woke up coughing and breathing but the stench was still absolutely overwhelming. Donny was in the same shape. Of course we had to ride in the back of the pickup going home and we rode along way in the back where we would get the most wind so we surmised we would have the entire stink blown off by the time we got home. Ahem, we were wrong. Mom wouldn't let us in the house and made us undress outside and bury our clothes. She placed some soap outside and told us to pick it up once she was back in the house and go down to the dam and lather up and swim it off and repeat for a couple hours. That didn't seem to do much for our smell so she fixed us each a plate of supper and set it out (kinda like feeding the dog) and called us to eat as she went back inside.

I don't remember how long this went on as the smell slowly subsided but it was weeks of being isolated because no one would get close to us. Even after it was what we thought gone every time we got wet it seemed to revive that awful smell. Anyway we had learned what a skunk was and never had a desire to tame one for a pet again.

The Rabbit Experiment

We had many more experiments left to explore in our educational development and one of those follows here. We had some rabbits that we got from Marion Rowton to raise for meat. Things were going well with the project but we had to keep them penned up because of the cats. Mom had plenty of cats and we were afraid they would kill the rabbits if we were to let them roam. Donny decided we should conduct a test so all three of us joined in on this research effort. We had a big buck rabbit in a cage by himself so we caught a big tomcat and decided to drop him in the cage and if he killed the rabbit we would skin it and have rabbit for supper and if the buck killed the cat we would bury it and Mom would never be the wiser.

Well the cat wasn't nearly as excited about the test as we were so he done quite a little damage to Donny's hide in his considerable resistance to being dropped through the hole in the top of the pen but with Donny's determination the cat was finally in and the hatch closed.

The excitement was instant; the buck took after the cat with his hind feet. They went around that cage so fast we could hardly tell which was which with the rabbit the aggressor and the cat looking for an exit. The cat actually at one point went the full length of the cage, running upside down on the wire on top with the rabbit flipping and hitting the top with both hind feet at the same time but mostly behind the cat. The cat was screaming to the point we were afraid Mom might hear so Donny finally opened the hatch and a round or two later the cat, I think accidently, hit it at full throttle and was out of sight in less than a second. We never saw that cat around that shed again. Anyway we had our answer so we were no longer in fear of letting the rabbits out occasionally without fear of them becoming cat food.

Electricity

In the early '50's a Rural Electric cooperative was formed in Circle called McCone Electric. In 1954 the power lines reached our area. We were so far and isolated from the main line that Dad couldn't afford to have them bring power to our place. However the Boulden brothers who ran the Mosby filling station and post office where we got our mail had a 32-volt generator with a battery bank to store power. They were right by the power transmission line so they hooked up and didn't need the generator. Dad was able to buy the generator set so he built a little "powerhouse" out of boards he helped Russell Rowton saw on his little lumber sawmill.

Uncle Clarence Rogge had power before with a wind charger and batteries for when the wind wasn't blowing so he knew how to wire for electricity. He came over and wired the house and even ran a wire to the icehouse which was becoming a bunkhouse. Soon there were used 32-volt appliances for sale or give away all over as more and more people got 110-volt power so Mom picked up some fixtures like a mixer and clothes iron and even a refrigerator. This meant the old icebox was now a cupboard "as it should always have been" and we didn't need the icehouse any longer so it was remodeled to a bunkhouse. Later on Dad even papered the inside ceiling with feed sacks to stop the dirt that came through between the logs on the roof before it reached our beds.

In our new bunkhouse we had one light fixture and bulb on the ceiling. Wow was that ever nice. The fixture had a pull chain for off and on so we ran a string from there to Donny and my double bed and one to Larry's single bed downstairs so we could turn on the light before heading out for the late night nature calls. What luxury the likes of which we'd never seen.

We did have one close call in the bunkhouse that I remember very well. We had a wood stove downstairs and Larry was the operator. One chilly evening he built a fire and warmed us up. When bedtime came he closed the chimney damper a little to slow the burn and not burn up the wood so fast. Sometime during the night I remember putting my head under my pillow and rubbing my face on the cool underside. I got to coughing and finally kind of came to or woke up and turned on the light. It was so smoky you couldn't even see the light or anything else; it was just a distant looking glow. I hollered to Larry who was sleeping soundly as the smoke hadn't got all the way down to his bed but it was close.

When he stood up he was in the smoke, it was that close to him. He got up and opened the door and eventually the smoke dissipated. I don't know if the damper was a little too closed or if there was a weather inversion that caused a back draft or maybe both but it was very nearly a tragedy.

The Great Hunt

Dad had an old 30-30 rifle that he carried in a scabbard on his saddle a lot of the time so it had been through a few horse wrecks. The stalk was so badly abused it looked more like an old piece of barn wood, including the slivers, than a gun stalk. We always called it the gun with the bent barrel but I'm sure that wasn't the case. It was the magazine that was bent a little instead. Anyway Larry was allowed to take it hunting and I was invited along in case he was to get a deer and would need help.

We headed out north of the house very early in the morning. Along the rim of the hayfield we spotted a mule deer doe. Larry took aim and knocked a front leg off her at the knee. She ran and we began "tracking" her. We soon ran out of blood drops but we kept on her tracks. She taught us a great deal that day. After about four miles of very rough country we found where her tracks turned right up a steep slope then turned right again and we found where she had been lying down. She had lain down where she could watch her tracks below where we came by about twenty yards from her. We then tracked her back to her and our previous track and she began backtracking. She came to the same washout she and we had jumped earlier. We jumped it again but soon discovered there were no fresh tracks over ours so we went back and jumped the washout.

We found that she had walked right up to the washout and then jumped at a 90-degree left angle about twelve feet up the hill. A very clever move for a three legged deer but we were back on track. She went over that hill to an oil well road following it for about a half mile then up the steep northern slope of the next ridge. We found that at the top she turned right along the rim so she could watch us tracking her down the road. This was getting to us that she was so much smarter than us and it was starting to get dark so we gave up and started our roughly five-mile trek home. It was well after dark when we made it home so needless to say there were some serious concerns going on and we were seriously reprimanded for causing the worry.

Jesus Christ

I'm not sure of the year but I believe it was the summer of 1954 that a small miracle happened in our community. A young lady named Delores Lindquist came to our area from Nebraska and offered a week of Bible school classes at the Mosby community hall. Mom heard about it and got us boys there each day to attend the classes. That was my first real exposure to our savior. I had heard of God and Jesus but that was usually when someone struck their thumb with a hammer. This opportunity was much more enlightening and comforting. I didn't have much opportunity to pursue any further study until high school. Donny and I then took instruction at the local Lutheran church under the direction of Pastor David Zietlow and were confirmed in the Lutheran Church Wisconsin Synod. I did stray away after high school for several years until in Lewistown I transferred into the Missouri Synod St Paul Lutheran Church where I am still a member.

Another Life-Changing Event

I had watched Dad for hours and hours over some time building a dam with a team and one man Fresno. He would walk behind running the handle to either fill it with dirt or in skid or travel mode then lift it to spread the three to five cubic feet of dirt onto the fill. When the dirt got too hard to load he would unhook the Fresno and hook up a one bottom plow and plow up the cut sections on both ends of the dam then start hauling dirt again. These fills did not settle with age. They were compacted better than current methods by the thousands of horse tracks for each tiny thin layer of new dirt.

Dad had leased the north section he owned to an oil company for possible oil and gas exploration and production. That summer they decided to drill an exploratory well so site development and road building began. I could hear the machinery from our house so out of curiosity I walked out there probably a mile or so away.

When I arrived there was a man running a 2U D8 with cable dozer removing the topsoil for a road. Oh MY Goodness that machine was just plowing through, moving more dirt in five seconds than Dad could in a day. I was absolutely mesmerized. I spent a few days walking along watching all this extraordinary progress and silently hoping the operator would invite me on board but that never happened. I was however totally hooked on pursuing the ability to run one of those monsters. I did just a few years after that but more on that later. They plugged the hole and never returned but they did not disclose what they found so it must have been a dry hole or not enough volume to make it profitable. But not all was lost as the compensation Dad received for the damages were sufficient for him to purchase a brand-new Case Model D tractor which replaced the old, old iron wheeled tractor he had for the prior two years.

Christmas

Christmas at our house was quite low-key. Mom would sometimes cut a cedar tree and put some homemade ornaments, paper mostly, and sometimes strings of popcorn. We had socks to hang and we usually got an orange, a tiny bit of candy, and gloves or socks or whatever Santa knew we needed. If there were essential items of clothing we needed it usually showed up as a Christmas present but Mom always managed to get us one toy each. It was normally a very insignificant item but a toy nevertheless. We treasured those gifts and took care of them so they would last until next Christmas. I remember one such gift that I received in the form of a light cardboard garage complete with a car lift and some paper autos and pickups.

I guarded that with my life and it lasted, if I remember right, almost three years before it was worn out or stepped on or some combination of catastrophic events.

POINTS TO PONDER

Must you stand down before you can stand up?

CHAPTER 5
FIRST JOBS
AND SCHOOL

Eighth Grade Graduation

My brothers graduated together from eighth grade one year ahead of me so in my eighth grade I was alone so the trips to and from school were quite boring. Dad had built a lean-to in the timber by the school for us to stall horses in if we wanted to ride to school so I decided to ride old Sox to school which I did. I took the bridle off and put a halter on her for the day. That night after school I took the halter off to put the bridle on and she jerked away from me and ran toward home. She would stop about every quarter mile and graze. I would approach her very slowly, talking gently. When I would get within ten feet or so she would take off for another quarter mile.

After about four of these sessions I was still talking to her but there was nothing gentle about my tone. When I got to the gate in the lane a quarter mile from home she was standing there waiting for me to open the gate. I wanted to kick her in the belly but my legs were not long enough. I opened the gate and she went to the barn and waited for me to unsaddle her. Needless to say I never rode to school again, walking was much less stressful. I did make it through the year graduating at twelve years old with the second highest test score in the county behind my classmate Donna.

First Full-Time Job

I was ready to get on someone's payroll so Larry got me a job with a neighbor about eighteen miles the way the crow flies due east. My job was to cook for a lambing crew. Dad took me over and dropped me off and the next day the whole lambing crew quit. No, it wasn't my fault, as I had not fixed them a meal yet. So, on my first day I got a promotion to a lambing job. I was happy as I was to be paid two dollars a day for cooking and, although there was no discussion with the boss, I knew the lambers that quit were getting five dollars a day so, wow, I was in the chips, big money!

The first week was some of everything; I milked goats, done some cooking and babysitting baby girls while their mom was out riding. We also pulled my new home, "a sheep wagon," out into some rolling timbered hills. The boss had purchased 350 head of bred yearling ewes and dumped them from a couple semis in the rolling hills with no fences at all. Of course the sheep didn't know the country (and neither did I) so they were restless and the party was about to start. It was spring with long daylight days so the sheep were on the move about 4:30 AM and wouldn't bed down before 9:30-10:00 o'clock at night. I had one horse and one dog that was smart but had obviously been abused so if I spoke in any kind of loud or threatening tone he would tuck his tail and head for the wagon regardless how far that was. The boss came out twice a week with a fresh horse as I could only get about three days out of a fresh one before they were wore down and I couldn't get them to move. It was a nightmare as the sheep were lambing all along the way. I had some tepees (three iron rods with a canvas cover) so I would put a newborn in there with the mother and then try to catch up with the band. I'd get back to the tepee maybe five, six, seven hours later and the side would be torn out and the lamb dead and mother long gone.

The neighbor to the west had put in a crop of oats early so it was maturing well when the sheep found it. It had a three barbed wire fence around it with a post about every forty feet and the wires touching the ground in between so the sheep could go through it at twenty miles an hour without ducking. I could not get them out as hard as I tried. The owner of the oats came by and he was not a happy camper. He did help me enough to get them out and thanks to the dog I was able to get them moving away. It was a daily challenge every day from then on trying to keep them away. Old Sam, the oats neighbor, was always packin' after that but he never threatened me and I didn't care what he done to the sheep at that point.

So I spent a year there one month. At twelve years old and never away from home before it was an awful long short month of twenty-six days. Dad came to pick me up and the boss wrote a check, folded it over, and handed it to me and we left for home. I knew I was rich now and maybe Dad could retire. After some time riding along I sneaked the check out of my pocket and took a glance. I went into shock as the check was in the amount of $42.00. Now don't get me wrong that was still a lot of money for me but it wasn't even the two dollars a day for the twenty-six days let alone the five dollars I assumed I was making which would have generated 130 dollars. I rode along in stunned silence for quite some time and finally got the courage to inform Dad of this terrible injustice.

I told him my sad story expecting the tires to start squealing as he stomped on the brakes to flip a U-turn to go back and demand justice or beat the guy up. Instead he listened patiently until I had finished then he calmly replied, "Yep, that education costs money no matter where you get it." I thought those were the cruelest words I'd ever heard. We continued on home in silence. Those words however turned out to be so profound as I grew older and life's events taught me many lessons without compensation. I always thought back to his remarks and appreciate them to this day.

Another bit of advice he gave me that has served me well: you can work fifty years building a good reputation and ruin it in five minutes.

My First Car

In the summer of 1956 I bought my first car from a neighbor, Easton Rowton. It was a well used model A Ford that I paid fifteen dollars down on with the promise to pay the ten-dollar balance after my lambs sold. It was pretty much original except the ignition switch had been modified to require a key which was with it. I drove it home, oh so proudly and of course showing it off to my brothers and taunting them a little about my good fortune. The next day Larry wanted to borrow it to run down to Warren Rowton's place. I told him absolutely not as I had hardly got to drive it myself. He didn't accept that rejection and continued to beg and insist. Finally I nodded my head in approval so he let me up and when I finally got my hand and arm removed from between my shoulder blades I gave him the key. The road to Rowtons was a two track road through cedar trees with many sharp curves and no visibility. On one of the curves he was speeding and he met Velma Moss in her pickup and she was also speeding in the oncoming direction. The ensuing crash wrecked the pickup and totaled the model A. Fortunately neither of them were seriously injured but when I got the news my pride was very seriously injured. This made making the final payment very painful as well.

Of course I didn't know it then but that was likely a lucky turn for me as at twelve years old and no driving experience I probably would have wrecked it soon anyway and the injury results could have been much worse.

My First County Fair

I got my first fair experience at the age of twelve in Lewistown, Montana. I am not sure how I got there but I remember everything else clearly. I had six dollars with me which was probably fifty percent or more of my entire net worth and I was excited to be "on my own" and ready for all a fair has to offer. I entered the gate into the midway and a very nice but very loud gentleman hollered at me and waved me over to his booth. He had a bunch of wooden rings that one could rent three of for fifty cents. If you got two of them over the wooden pins sticking up you would win prizes. He set a nice stuffed animal on the counter. I tried and failed so he quickly added another fine one so I could get both. Again I failed and he kept putting up more and more and kept encouraging me that I was so close. At some point he even added a wristwatch to the growing stack. Wow, a wristwatch and all those other "things;" I couldn't quit now.

Well soon my pockets were empty and I had nothing. When he seen I was broke he didn't even acknowledge that I was still standing there. He began shouting to someone behind me and waving them in as he removed all the prizes I was "so close" to winning from the counter. I walked off in stunned silence and a huge lump in my throat to spend the rest of the day walking around with my hands in my empty pockets watching the other kids having a blast on all kinds of rides.

Of course I didn't know it at the time but that turned out to be a very fortunate incident. To this day I have never again spent another dime on those scams. If I would have "won" I would have likely squandered much more than six dollars over the years. Dad was right again, education costs money no matter where you get it!

High School

When high school was about to start in the fall of 1956 Donny and I moved into a little house that Dad rented for us in Winnett and we began "batching." Donny was fourteen and I was twelve and small for my age so he was sorta the "boss" (or at least thought he was). Dad would also, at the first of each month, give the local grocery store twenty-five dollars. This debit allowed us to get that amount of groceries for the month. If we needed more we had to pay for it ourselves so this taught us to be very frugal. If we wanted to eat hot lunch at school we had to buy our own tickets and at thirty-five cents a day each that ate up our earned discretionary funds quickly, which made it tough to come up with the twenty-five cent admittance fee to the theater for the weekly movie let alone the ten cents for popcorn.

We started high school together taking some of the same classes that first year. Being young and small I was afraid of not fitting in so I signed up to play football. Yea I know, but somehow at the time it seemed rational. Please consider I had never seen a football let alone a game if that helps.

I wasn't big enough to be a ninety-eight-pound weakling as I only weighed eighty-eight pounds soaken wet with all my clothes on, that's the only way you showered in high school at twelve years old, is with all your clothes on. I never did get any hair on my chest.

At our football orientation all the "football" players were assembled in the gym by the coach. After a short briefing we went to the locker room, seniors first in line followed by juniors, sophomores and freshmen. There was a large pile of equipment and uniforms in the middle of the floor. Those big old seniors got first pick and down the line it went to me last. There wasn't much left so I didn't have to sort much like they did, I just took one of each of what I seen the others taking.

The fitting was a bit of a problem for me. If I tucked the jersey in you couldn't see the numbers and if I left it out I couldn't run. Everyone else had knee length pants but mine were ankle length which put some of the built-in protections in cumbersome places. The pants didn't fit all that bad except they were a little loose around the armpits but as long as I kept my elbows clinched down they would stay up. So I was ready to hit the field.

The Play

I don't want to dwell on football but I do want to mention "the play" of that first year. I call it "the play" because it was the only play they ran that year while I was in the game. We were on offense so when we broke the huddle no one went to the right side so I did. I don't remember what the play was now, but that should come as no surprise, as I didn't remember what it was then either.

You see the others had holes in the sides of their helmets over their ears so they could hear the quarterback. Mine had those holes too but mine were down under my jaw on my neck so I couldn't understand him. He sounded like he was trying to shout at us with a mouthful of watermelon without drooling.

Anyway there were six of us and two had gone out to the left then there was the halfback, the quarterback and the wetback. That wasn't really his position; we just called him that because the quarterback drooled on him all the time.

When they hiked the ball I ventured a bit further out to the right as I didn't want to get in the way and get someone hurt. I then turned and looked back to see what was happening and lo and behold here comes the football. The crazy quarterback had thrown the ball to me! It was not a perfect pass as there was a defensive guy in the backfield harassing him that had managed to come across unchecked somehow. I suppose someone missed an assignment. The ball was well above the numbers but right in the chest wasn't that bad under those conditions.

Then a small miracle happened, mostly out of self defense, I caught the ball. I then panicked as I had seen what defenses do to the guy with the ball. So, it was decision time, what should I do? I decided to run for my life and took off. I had a fifty-fifty chance of going the right direction and I got lucky. (A friend on the sideline told me later it looked like I was trying to carry a large leather suitcase with no handle). The coach had told us not to worry about what's going on behind you, just concentrate on what's ahead. Well there wasn't anything ahead of me except goalposts so I decided I better look back and see what dangers might exist behind me and when I turned my head everything went black, so I reached up with my free hand and turned my helmet so I could see. Sure enough there was danger lurking. There was a defender only about thirty yards back and I could see the deadly sneer on his face and could hear him breathing. (I found out later he was a big old ninety-one-pound sophomore with asthma, which explains why I could hear him breathing from that distance.) It was about here where I realized I had worked up a sweat as I could feel it running down my leg. I also realized how much danger I was in so I quickly developed a survival plan. There were these white lines painted across the field so the next one I came to I tripped over it, fell down, and crawled up under my shoulder pads with only part of the football and one wet shoe sticking out. As you can tell it worked out as I'm still here and able to write about it.

There are two things I never did figure out about that day. Why did the coach put me in and why, after such an outstanding performance, did he take me out?

I was again an observer from the bench. I excelled at that position as well and soon became an advisor to the coach. I would advise him on such things as when I was back with the dry towels or fresh water, etc.

Freshman Year

The first year of high school was fairly uneventful. We took mostly basic courses like English, advanced math for me and algebra for Donny, biology, history and other boring "opportunities." The little house we had was quite basic as well. We had electricity and a wood stove. It was a two room setup so the stove was near the entryway between the two so it would heat both. That was however, strictly a theory, as when it was cold it done neither. We had a water bucket that we packed water in from a spigot near the alley and when we forgot to dump it at night it would freeze solid and the bottom swelled so bad we had to put a book (my homework) under one side so it didn't tip over. It made the comments of an old salty local gentleman by the name of Jim Green ring true. He always said that on those cold brisk mornings he would build a raging hot fire in his heating stove then run outside and get on the downwind side of his cabin and catch some of the heat as it went by!

During the year we both worked "odd" jobs (I'm not sure whether the odd meant us or the job). One of those was unloading coal. Vernon Bauer had a semi and he was contracted to haul the heating coal from the Roundup coal mine to the Winnett School. The trailer had no "dump" capabilities so the coal had to be shoveled off. We jumped on that opportunity as it paid cash. It was not boring either as each of us, as we shoveled, was counting the others scoops to make sure we got the five-dollar contract fee split equitably. It took four different handlings of the coal to get it from the front of the trailer to the slide into the coal bin in the basement of the elementary school. We didn't always get done in one night, unless he told us we had to, but when finished we would go to Tiffs Bar where he was relaxing and he would pay us.

We had a few other evening jobs now and then but almost always had weekend jobs either helping Dad on the ranch, or when we could, working for other ranchers for cash.

On another occasion we were helping reroof one of George Orr's houses. It had wooden shingles and they were badly split and the nails were coming loose, it was definitely time. One morning I had the job of running the skill saw to cut the old shingles at four inches in from each end so we could put a new one x four on to have a solid edge for the new roofing to adhere to. It was chilly and I had on a pair of old gloves that were too big for me. As I was cutting, a shingle came loose in front of the saw and was binding a little so I reached up with my left hand to grab it out of the way and the saw blade caught the end of the thumb and *kerchunk* it took my thumb with it up under the shield and stopped the saw. It happened so fast I still had the trigger pulled and the saw was just going hummmmmmmmm.

Back to Aunt Ferns' and she rushed me over to Roundup for triage. I thought the accident hurt but when I got in the doctor's office and the nurse took a toothbrush to the wound to get the sawdust out with no anesthesia I knew what pain really was. It had split the thumb from the tip through the side of the thumbnail down to the first joint where it damaged the tendon that still shows a knot and is sensitive to pressure. I was very fortunate that it healed without lasting effects of significance.

Fern could relax now for a couple of paragraphs until Donny cuts his fingers off!

POINTS TO PONDER

Must you shape down before you can shape up?

CHAPTER 6
SMALL TOWN, USA

S MALL TOWNS IN the 1950s were much different than most towns today. They had their own character and personality. Ours was Winnett. The little town in this story had three bars and a tavern along with two churches, a movie theater, a drug store, a hotel, and Ethel's. Ethel was a short stout woman. To give you an idea of her appearance imagine a fifty-five-gallon barrel sitting atop a pair of worn out army boots with a dress pulled tightly over it and a pumpkin with a dust mop on top. The little bulges weren't exactly in the right places but I think you get the picture.

Ethel's place was pretty much the "city" center and Ethel done pretty much everything. She was the gas pumper, the waitress, the shelf stocker for the grocery section, the preacher, the postmistress, the tire changer, the swamper, the coffee maker, the telephone operator, the windshield washer, occasional barber, the doctor, the lawyer, the engineer and everything else that needed done. I don't know if she graduated from grade school or not and she didn't have any formal degrees of any kind hanging on the walls but she was extremely talented, resourceful, and efficient.

I thought the location of her enterprise was because that was the only place in town they had hit a gasoline well and a kerosene well and a water well all in one place. I would learn about buried tanks later.

Some examples of her efficiencies follow. As stated, she was the postmistress so when she sorted the mail she would read all the postcards then throw them in a box. Then when she was running the telephone switchboard and listening to all the details and overheard someone that had a postcard coming she would simply tell them what the message was as well as adding some detail that the writer may have left out in their brevity. So if a postal inspector had ever found our little town, stamps would still be a nickel as the mail only had to go halfway, cutting costs considerably.

She would then use these discarded cards as receipts when people bought gas. This was not only efficient, it was a little like the lottery as every so often someone would get a personalized receipt.

She was the shelf stocker and I seen one day she had canned peas and hominy with dust all over the tops. I asked her why she stocked these items. Her response was that no one ever bought any of them so that saved her considerable time in not having to restock! Now that's innovation and efficiency at its best.

Also when gassing up a vehicle she would check the oil with her grease rag then wipe the windshield with the same rag. This was efficient because it kept the bugs from sticking to the windshield, saving her time when they stopped in again. She also used the same rag to wipe the counter where the coffee club (a gang of old geezers) hung out telling lies and spilling coffee. Her coffee always had a slick on top of it but they drank it anyway.

I remember one time one of the geezers that always had a cigar butt in his mouth had it burnt pretty short but he lit it again anyway and it dropped out of his mouth into his coffee cup and it ignited. It was a tin cup so it didn't break and as soon as the slick burned off it went out. The startled coffee drinker thought this was great as it should have warmed up his coffee. Well as stated, it may have, but the tin cup got extremely hot so he burnt his lips and tongue so he had scabs for quite awhile.

On another occasion old Clem came in one morning for coffee and BS and he looked terrible. Very pale and moving very slowly. Ethel asked him what was wrong and he said he was constipated, had been for two days. Well Ethel grabbed a piece of paper and pencil and asked him how far it was home. He told her it was six miles, she then asked how many gates, and he said two. What's your average speed on that dirt road? "About fifteen miles an hour," was his reply. She took that info and headed into the back room. She came back with a small jug and ordered him to take two teaspoons of it and head home immediately. He did as she said and didn't return for a couple of days. When he did return Ethel asked him how things "worked out." He replied, "You're a fine doctor but not so good as an engineer, you missed the outhouse by seventy-five feet!"

Another time I recall when I was present a geezer was telling a whopper and needed the use of both arms to accentuate the point of his story and accidently tipped the coffee pot over so the coffee was spreading across the counter. Fortunately Ethel came in from checking someone's oil with the grease rag so she was able to corral the spilt coffee, because the rag wouldn't soak up any, and herd it back into the pot so no harm no foul, they were able to finish the pot before the story was finished. This was just another example of her efficient moments.

First Full Summer Job

When school got out in the spring of '57 I went to work for Lyle and Max Kimble on their ranch where I used to help ride on the Musselshell River east of Cat Creek. I was paid $2.50 per day or $75.00 a month. My days started early as I had to gauge the oil well tanks nearby before breakfast each morning and breakfast was at 6:00 AM. I did all regular ranch work like riding, branding, haying, fencing, etc.

There were a few things that stand out for me about that summer. One was when Lyle and Max went to the fair in Billings for three days and left me doing some haying. That was before swathers so we cut the hay with a side mount cycle bar mower on a 9N Ford tractor and raked it into windrows with a side delivery rake that was run by the power take off shaft from the tractor. The seat cushion was worn out on the old tractor so we had an old blanket folded up on it to make it a little more comfortable. The next day after they left it was a bit chilly so I put on my coveralls and began raking. When the sun got a little higher I was getting too warm but I didn't want to stop so I stood up and took my coveralls off down to my waist and tucked them under me on the blanket. I was merrily bouncing along when suddenly someone jerked the blanket out from under me! I was startled and quickly looked back to see who was there thinking that was something one of my brothers might do. When I seen what had really happened I was almost in shock. The blanket had caught on the drive shaft and wrapped around it and the sleeves of my coveralls were bouncing on the blanket but the blanket had it covered enough there was nothing for them to hook onto so my life was spared. Needless to say I learned a whole lot about safety that day that I've never forgotten.

Another not so fun chore I recall was after threshing the alfalfa seed crop we had to weigh the bags. The scale they had only went to 250 pounds. The sacks wouldn't set on it by themselves so someone had to hold them to be weighed. I was the only one light enough to not exceed the gross weight limit while holding the 110 to 120 pounds so; I was left holding the bag, while they read the scale and deducted my ninety-six pounds for an accurate net weight.

It wasn't all work, however, as the river was close by and I liked to fish. I had setlines out all the time and if we didn't have to work after supper I would check them. I caught so many catfish that Max wouldn't let me bring anymore to the house so I started releasing them in a nearby pond that was fed by a warm water artesian well so it had good aquatic life for them to feed on. I never did fish in it but heard later others did and the fish had done well. One of the ones I put in there weighed twenty-two pounds so it could have got quite heavy but I don't know.

Donny worked that summer up the river several miles for Johnny Hill doing much the same as I.

Second Vehicle

That fall I had a little money and Lloyd Berg at Berg Ford in Winnett had a little pickup for sale. It was a well maintained 1935 Chevy. I was thirteen by then so I couldn't get a driver's license yet. Donny however had turned fifteen and got his license so I let him drive when we were in town. It served us pretty well but I think it was probably designed for forty-five to fifty miles an hour and I liked sixty to seventy much better. That resulted in the rods going out near the Cat Creek turnoff. We got it drug home to the old homestead and Donny pulled the engine and tore it down. He concluded the crankshaft was ruined and we didn't know where to get parts and I couldn't afford them anyway so we were afoot again.

I don't remember for sure but I believe it was later that winter when Donny got his first car. It was a 1950 Ford four door that John Marty had traded in at Berg Ford. Wow, what luxury. It had a flat head V8 engine with two water pumps. We couldn't afford antifreeze so we had to drain the radiator and engine every night.

The water pumps did not completely drain so some mornings the tiny bit of ice in the bottom would stick the impellers for a few seconds and cause the belt to slip and squeal. One cold morning that happened but didn't quit in a few seconds so Donny reached in and grabbed the belt to try to get it turning. Just then the pumps turned loose and the belt took three of his fingertips through the V pulley and cut them off. Two of them were still attached by a bit of skin on the bottom side. We went up to Aunt Fern's again for help. Donny wanted her or me to cut or pull the skin loose but Fern insisted we wrap his hand and she took him to Lewistown for care. They were able to reattach the two and it was quite successful considering the shape they were in. He did have trouble with the fingernails the rest of his life but he was glad he had the fingers.

One of the quirks of the Ford was the headlights would go out sometimes. Donny knew where the problem was but the only time he would work on them was at night doing sixty miles an hour down the highway. I recall one incident just after we crossed the old Mosby Bridge which was very narrow with the overhead super structure the lights went out. Instantly Donny disappeared down under the dash keeping one hand on the steering wheel. When he made his move I think it put pressure on his gas pedal leg as I'm sure we were gaining speed! When I heard the sweet clover and grass hitting my side I would say, "Your way a little," and likewise if it was his side it was "my way a little." Soon he needed both hands so I reached over to steer, fortunately the lights soon came on and we hadn't gained more than five miles an hour so as soon as I started breathing again all was well.

On another occasion we three brothers went to a Saturday night dance at the Flatwillow hall. By the time the dance was over none of us were feeling any pain but Donny in particular was plum numb. Donny got the car going and went the wrong direction, east instead of west. We talked him into turning around so he backed off the road. It so happened the county had been mining gravel and there was a five foot straight down bank near the road. Donny dropped both hind wheels over the cliff. There were five of us in the car so four of us got out and went down the bank to see if we could lift the car enough to get some traction. We did and it did but Donny had a lot of RPMs going and the cascade of gravel shooting out behind both wheels would have been deadly had one of us been that far out on the edge. So now we're not stuck any longer but Donny is still behind the wheel. In the course of trying to talk him down he explained, "I've drunk drover'n this" which pretty much made our point.

Finally we got Larry behind the wheel but about halfway back to Winnett the lights went out (imagine that)! Larry didn't have the practice Donny did so he ran off the road but it was a gentle slope. We finally got Donny awake enough to fix the "problem" but he was sleepy enough by then that he no longer protested Larry being our chauffeur.

Sophomores

We went back to the same "house" the second year. The everyday grind was much the same drill as last year. School and work kept us out of mischief so that wasn't all bad. School was going pretty well but it seemed I always had homework and Donny seldom did. When he did have, it took him a few minutes to complete and it took me a few hours. I didn't complain to him because I was afraid he'd quit helping me when I needed it.

Algebra was a real challenge for me. I tried to explain to the instructor all winter long that you were supposed to use numbers for math not the alphabet but he couldn't get it through his head. He insisted that X times Y should equal Z, go figure! That never happened for me.

I think he might have been the one that came up with the report cards they used.

They had an A, B, C, D and F, no E which I figured would have stood for Excellent which is where I was between the D and F. They never used the B and A on my card so I assumed they stood for B-elow A-verage which, of course, wouldn't apply to me.

He did have some math skills though as he averaged fourteen F's and came up with a D-. In retrospect I think he intentionally made that mathematical error so I wouldn't be in his class again next year embarrassing him in front of a new class for his lack of understanding the difference between the numbers and letters issue.

POINTS TO PONDER

Must you screw down before you can screw up?

CHAPTER 7
FINISHING SCHOOL

Another Move for Our Parents

In the early spring of 1958, our folks moved again. Dad took a job managing a ranch for an absentee landowner on the lower Musselshell River. Dad wanted to leave room for Brother Larry to operate his place along with Grandpa Petersen's place when he got out of the Navy.

This meant the folks got a "new" house. It was a two room log house about sixty years old with most of the same amenities as the two room log house they left behind. It did have electricity from a power line instead of from a battery. This meant they could get rid of the old battery powered static machine and replace it with a snow machine. This was quite an operation as they had to put up a chicken roost high above the roof on a metal pipe. It was too far up for the chickens to fly to so I never did see a chicken use it. They ran a wire from it down to a crack by the kitchen window and inside to the snow machine. This was quite a machine with a window in front to watch the snowstorm in. It also had a built-in static maker. Dad could come in for lunch on a good hot day and flip on the snow machine and watch a good snowstorm. Occasionally it sounded like someone was trying to say something inside it but the static was able to prevail.

My little sister Diane was born that fall in October after we had started our junior year. I was fourteen at the time and never home other than occasional weekends so I didn't really get to know her well until she got out of high school. She came and stayed with us for a short time while working in Lewistown which was a real treat for us and we got much better acquainted.

Contractors

The summer of 1958 was another learning experience. Donny and I decided to become contractors. We gave the Brown ranch a price for building a mile or so of four wire fence west of Sand Springs. That went well so we moved farther east and agreed to stack hay bales and grain bundles for Clem Larson on his ranch/farm east of Sand Springs. I had acquired a 1950 Ford pickup with an unsynchronized four-speed transmission. That was an excellent teaching tool for learning the value of the clutch and RPM combination. After some practice it was almost easier to shift without the clutch after getting going if you weren't on a heavy pull. Anyway we were to get seven cents a bale for stacking the hay in the stackyards. Clem furnished an old tractor and a wooden slip that drug along flat on the ground. We would take turns driving the tractor pulling alongside the bales and the other would snag them with the hay hooks and drag them onto the "sled" or slip as it was called. We had to then stack them on the slip until it was hard to drag (I think we went about four tiers high then to the stack where we hand carried them up the "stairs" of bales to get thirteen rows high). I recall one incident when we had caught up with the baler and I snagged a bale that had about a foot of a live snake sticking out the side of the bale and he was quite upset with the situation. After I settled back down to where my feet were back on the sled I carefully stacked that bale on the outside and when we put it up on the haystack we put him on the outside row on the sunny side. He was pretty limber when we got back with the next load.

We fixed fence for Clem whenever we couldn't stack hay because of weather or other interruptions in the process. We used his old cab over jeep for that project and that was kinda fun seeing how far a four-wheel drive could go.

We went to the Sand Springs store one night with my pickup to get some sodas and other minor necessities and on the way back the differential on my pickup started going out. It got us back but was extremely noisy. The next night Donny took it apart and it needed almost everything, spider gears, bearings and I think even the ring gear and pinion. A few days later when Clem made a parts run for the ranch he picked up all the parts we needed with the cost to be deducted from our contract. Donny got it all reassembled within a few nights and asked me to start it and run it for a bit while still up on blocks with the cover off the differential so he could listen and look to see that all was well. It was, for about a minute, then due to no lubrication it squealed and froze up solid. Oh boy, what a disappointment that was. We'd been afoot for a couple weeks already and now we needed almost all the same parts again. Dad's words floated heavy in my mind again, "that education costs money no matter where you get it."

We were to get two cents a bundle to stack the grain bundles. He needed them stacked in one place so when the threshing machine got there in the fall they could set up in one place and complete the whole project. We used a hayrack for that process pulled by the same tractor.

When we got all done we went in to "settle up" on our contract. We went over everything and then Clem asked if we had re-fenced the hay stacks, which he knew we hadn't. We told him no as that was not part of the deal. He explained that we were to stack the bales in the stack yards and they were not stack yards unless they were fenced. We spent almost another week fencing all the yards under close supervision. They obviously hadn't had that kind of attention in thirty or forty years. "Education," it's a wonderful thing!

Juniors

That fall of 1958 I got my long-awaited dream job working for Hugh Brindley running his old D7 Caterpillar with cable dozer and scraper on some evenings but mostly weekends until the ground froze too hard. I got an hourly wage and I don't remember what that was when I started but I think it was seventy-five cents. (He didn't know it but I would have done that job for nothing at the time.) I worked for him for over a year but not steady of course as I had school and frozen ground at times. We built dams, roads, dikes, leveled land, etc. Good experience to say the least.

I don't know why we didn't have the same house as the last two years but we moved to a different house. It had most of the same amenities as the last one like the outdoor toilet, wood stove, and two rooms. It did have an indoor sink in the kitchen but no water.

That fall we again entered the "how many outdoor toilets can you tip over on Halloween night" project. I don't know which team won as there was always lying going on about the success rate. One repeat "customer" got a step ahead of the tip over team as he moved his toilet ahead about three feet so it sat in front of the hole instead of over it. The three-man team that snuck rapidly up behind that particular toilet didn't see the hole and all three sort of, what you might say, "stepped in it." Fortunately I wasn't on that team and none of them were physically injured but were psychologically affected for some time.

I am sure however, that Donny and I won the contest of how many times one toilet could be tipped over. Every morning for nine straight days after Halloween when we went out to use our facility it was flat on its back. It was a matter of tipping it back up and realigning it on the hole. It was getting a bit creaky by then and on the tenth morning it was on its back but from the door it had folded out both ways with all four sides laying flat on the ground. We had to hurry to school for the rest of the week until we could rebuild it on the weekend. For what reason it wasn't turned over again we'll never know. I've always had my suspicions on culprits but no one has ever stepped up to claim their prize.

We had some venturous and prankster classmates that came up with some "great" ideas to torment others. Examples are when Ronnie Daum lit a ballpoint pen on fire with a cigarette lighter and stuck the smoldering remains in through the vent cover in the boy's bathroom. Someone had pulled the smoke alarm before we got back to the study hall and the stink was absolutely unbearable so we were ordered to evacuate and it took till noon the next day before the stink was tolerable enough to reenter the school. (I should have removed that cover at the last all school reunion to see if the butt of the pen was still there! Maybe next time.)

The south end of the study hall had a partial wall across with big openings on both ends and all the walls behind it had shelving which housed all the books for the school library. Some one of the geniuses attending school that year (not me I don't think) came up with yet another very impressive stunt. We borrowed some bobbins from the home ec room and would take the string and pull four or five books out on a shelf to where they were about to drop out on the floor. We would wrap the string around them and unwind it back to our desk. When everyone was seated and all was quiet with the study hall teacher observing all present you could very gently pull slowly on the string until the loud crash from the library occurred. You then wound the string up around your hand without showing any movement to others and thus remove the evidence. Very effective at keeping the study hall teacher on her toes and alert and picking up books and numerous students giggling, quite quietly of course.

Donny was getting into some very strange things in school by this time like calculus, trigonometry, chemistry, geometry, etc. I stuck with Algebra 1 myself.

Donny had played with cigarettes before but now was actually smoking regularly. I didn't approve, but that might have been jealousy on my part as I tried one big puff and went into convulsions coughing so I wasn't "man" enough, and I never got enough courage to try it again. (Lucky me.)

I played football and basketball that year. Donny played basketball but his niche was track. He was very good at the 880 and 440 yard runs. He really stood out in the former. I stood out in most of my plays but for all the wrong reasons!

Senior Year

When school started that fall I was sitting in the study hall waiting to get our orientation when a beautiful freshmen brunette walked in. I was smitten with her at first sight. I got to know her and we dated all year. She and her wonderful family were Lutherans and I was able to attend church with them. This led to both Donny and I being trained, baptized, and confirmed into the Lutheran church. God works in mysterious ways sometimes.

We started our senior year after a summer of me moving dirt for Hugh, and Donny worked all summer as well for the Bohn ranch.

I had acquired an old army 4x4 and we had put a homemade "camper" on it. We decided to save Dad some money and just stay in it all year. Our Uncle Benny Bentley and Aunt Elsie let us unload it in their yard near their garage. They left their back door unlocked so we could use their bathroom. SOOOO!! We finally had an indoor bathroom; the only catch was we had to go outside to get to it.

We ran an extension cord from the garage to the "camper" and Donny installed a pull string light fixture so we would have some light. The light also served as the sole heat source in the tiny room, so when we shut the light off our breath became the sole source. However the latter heat source for the night also created a lot of humidity so in the mornings when it was cold (which seemed like most of the time) our covers would be frozen to the wall and the ceiling would be frosted. This created another dilemma as when we turned the lightbulb on and it began to warm up it would proceed to "rain" inside, which when a drop hit the lightbulb it exploded. We solved this problem by cutting a coffee can in half and nailing it to the wall as an umbrella over the bulb. That did resolve the exploding problem but also cut the already limited light considerably. Oh well I didn't really want to see my homework anyway.

Uncle Benny and Aunt Elsie were very good to us in many ways including having us in for supper almost nightly which was a blessing as we had no microwave or stove so our diet, on our own, was pretty much beanie weenies or cold cereal with either frozen or warm milk depending on the weather.

Late that fall I turned sixteen so was ready for a driver's license, finally! I didn't have a vehicle worthy of a driving test so I borrowed a red and white '59 Ford from Stella Getten, and parked it just east of the courthouse door. I was nervous of course but I did pass the written exam. The patrolman said let's go for a ride so he followed me out the door. I got in the car and he went around back and asked me to turn on the left signal light. I looked down to comply and went into a panic. There hanging from the lever was a "sap" or night stick. I realized then that I had got into the sheriff's red and white '59 Ford. The keys were in the ignition so it was decision time. He checked all the lights so that gave me a little think time. Should I just steal the sheriff's car and take the patrolman for a ride as we weren't going to be gone long at all so it probably wouldn't be missed and save me the embarrassment. Then I thought what if the sheriff get's an emergency call, things could go south in a hurry for me. So as the patrolman opened the passenger door to get in common sense prevailed and I said I'm sorry but this is the wrong car. His response was, "Do you know which one is the right car?" I said "yes" and got out and three cars down was the "right" car and being exactly the same color and model I think helped lessen his reaction to my tragic error. By the way the sheriff's car passed the safety check!

Benny also was a hunter and fisherman and he included me in many of his adventures. I didn't have a rifle so he loaned me a 270 pump action that belonged to his brother-in-law. I became a very good marksman and I remember on one outing on the Musselshell River bottom when him and I got in a contest of shooting Cock Pheasant's heads off with those 270's. We took turns as opportunities presented themselves and the first one to miss was the loser. We had our limit when I missed so he won but it was fun.

We had a big buck contest each fall in high school where participation cost one dollar. I entered every year and I had never won. I was now a senior and this was my last chance. Benny knew this and we went out a few times without any luck.

He then arranged an outing with several others that I knew. We went down the Musselshell and hunted several different bottoms. A shooter or two would be stationed up on the bluff and the rest of the crew would "drive" the bottom on foot to scare the deer out toward the shooters. We had some pretty good success but I had nothing to show for it. We ended up on the lower Musselshell on the Taylor brothers place. I was designated a shooter so I climbed the bluff to where I could see the entire width of the peninsula they were to "drive." I learned a lot from that experience. The "drivers" were banging sticks on trees, singing, whistling, etc. to "scare" the deer out. From my vantage point I could see many deer moving around in front of the drivers, but with all the noise they knew where everyone was so they simply snuck back between them. I asked them all later if they had seen any deer and not one had seen any of the deer that passed back by them within ten to fifteen feet at times.

There was but one bunch that made a break for the coulee beside me and there was a very large whitetail buck with them. They were running flat out and I had learned to shoot with Dad's old 30-30 so I led him too much and shot in front of him the first time but the second shot was deadly and he collapsed within twenty yards. He was a dandy; five on one side and four on the other.

I won the contest with his over 200 pound field dressed weight. I mounted the horns and gave them to Benny.

Benny died of a heart attack the next spring and those horns hung on the wall there for years before Elsie moved out and I got them back.

I've had them displayed in my garage until the fall of 2017 when I gave them to my grandson, Brian Amundson, in Minnesota.

I will be forever grateful to Benny for his inclusion of me in so many ways and I still think of him often after all these years especially when I see those horns.

Later, after sharing what I had observed with the other hunters, I suggested that it might be a better strategy to be very quiet as you "drive" as then they could smell you but not know just where you are. We tried that theory with much more success in later outings so the deer educated me well that day.

Senior Year Sports

I had grown a bit and was now fifteen years old so I went out for football again and actually played the games (finally). I was now the wetback so about all I done on offense was try to protect the quarterback. Donny was doing a lot of running in preparation for the spring track season.

Our basketball team was less than stellar but we had fun. No buses in those days in our school district so there were many a cramped trip in overcrowded cars getting to and from games but I admire the loyal parents for all the sacrifices they made for us as our parents didn't attend any games and didn't even own a car.

Donny did extremely well in track that spring. I think he won every 880 (half mile) race he entered that year. St. Leo's had a good half miler as well but he always came in just behind Donny so when the district tournament arrived they had a plan. Donny had a habit of having to lead the entire race and always did. They decided they could use this against him so they entered their very good sprinter in the half mile along with their 880 star.

When the starting gun sounded the sprinter got the jump on Donny, but by the first turn in the oval track Donny passed him. We could see the setup so the coach and I were both screaming at Donny to slow down. He did not slow down so as he left the sprinter in the dust he just angled off into the infield and sat down to watch. Donny kept that pace and caught the last guy in the group before hitting the finish line way ahead of everyone else, setting a new record in the process, so their scheme backfired and put Donny in the record books! He caught a cold before the state track meet and did participate but couldn't breathe very well so he didn't win that one.

Great-Grandmother

My great-grandmother, Ina Howard Rothwell (1881-1973), lived in Great Falls. She was in her nineties and didn't drive. She had caught a ride with a relative down to spend some time with her daughter (my grandmother) "little" Ina as she was affectionately called by all that side of the family. When it was time for her to return home I, for some reason, was selected to drive her there with grandma's 1956 Chevy car. I had met her a few times but never got to know her so this was a very enjoyable ride. She was quite talkative and I learned a great deal about her of which unfortunately I've forgotten much of. One story has stuck with me as I think of it every time we travel that route. We were going along Otter Creek and she pointed out a scar angling up the bluff on the east side. It was steep and had many spots where someone had stacked flat rocks from the hillside to make "retaining walls" to get the trail wide enough for team and wagons. They were going to Brussett down near Jordan to prove up on a homestead. She said they traversed that hill one night in the rain with the team and covered wagon. She also said the wagon was leaking severely so everything and everyone inside were soaken wet and the kids were crying. They parked for the night on top the ridge and the wood was all wet so they couldn't get a fire going so it was a very long night. She then said, "They talk about the good old days, well they can have 'em!"

Flammable

One afternoon after school a classmate of mine invited me to ride along with him in his dad's tanker truck to haul a load of crude oil from the Bigwall oil field near Roundup to the refinery in Billings so I did. We had to gauge the tank before and after loading. The before went fine but it took long enough to load that it got dark on us. We couldn't find a flashlight and we couldn't see the crude on the steel tape without light. There were no smoking and flammable signs a plenty so we decided that once we could find where the oil started on the tape we would pull it way back from the hole in the top of the tank and I would light a match so he could see the markings on the tape. All went as planned until I lit the match.

Kaboom! The fire flew and the tank bulged loudly twice as it belched and tried to breathe. Why it didn't totally explode and come apart and blow us to smithereens only God knows. In two steps we were all the way down the ladder and running. It continued to burn wildly out of the open hole but no more explosions so he jumped in the truck and moved it a considerable distance away and walked back. We decided it must not be going to explode so we ran up the ladder and he slammed the lid down, latched it and we ran for our lives. The tank moaned and groaned a bit but no more fire just smoke seeping out around the lid.

There is no question God had his arms wrapped around two idiots that day and kept us safe through another learning moment.

Another Tragedy

One day in December I was invited to go with a small group in Jimmy Bohn's dad's new Buick car to Grass Range. For some reason, that I can't recall, I ended up not going. It wasn't long before word came back that there had been a head-on collision on a very dusty county road known as Elk Creek Road. Jimmy, who was driving, perished at the scene and the others were seriously injured with cuts and bruises.

Jimmy was a very likeable and athletic young man in his junior year of school.

His basketball skills were envied by all and the upcoming season had the high expectations of success. Donny and I were very much honored to be asked to be pallbearers and of course we accepted but that was a very difficult task at that age and being such good friends with Jimmy.

After healing from that traumatic event, we then had a good senior year. We had a respectable basketball season, which would have likely been a stellar season with Jimmy, a good senior prom, and we graduated with signed diplomas! It was the best we could do, all things considered.

WIT

The WIT is still well known in and around Central Montana. The Western Invitational Tournament was established in 1940 and though delayed during the Second World War, continued for fifty-five years. Sponsors would put together basketball teams made up of top college athletes. This of course started bringing in professional team scouts from all over the country (and beyond). This naturally brought more and more of the top players in the country to "get noticed."

I remember many but especially Nate Archibald who went on to an amazing pro career along with many others such as Phil Jackson, Mel Daniels, Dennis Rodman, John Stockton, Mark Eaton, Maurice Cheeks, David Robinson, Jack Gillespie, Craig Finberg, Doug Hashley, Bill Pilgeram, Jack O'Conner, Larry Krystowiak, and too many more to remember.

This event became a nationwide annual event for both prospective participants and good loyal basketball retirees and spectators. It took at least sixteen teams to make this work for two-loss outs and get through it in the allotted time.

If my memory serves me (and there is much doubt there) in about 1961 a team had to cancel very late. I was still participating occasionally with the Winnett town team. We were asked to enter a team to make the brackets complete. We had three men that had any potential of competing with this caliber of players. I was not one of them but I was asked to get on the roster to complete the team.

The first game was nothing more than humiliating. I was assigned to guard a six-foot ten-inch tall and probably 300-pound power forward from Minnesota. Needless to say, he was able to literally run over me physically and make it look so easy he didn't even get a whistle (except for his fans in the crowd).

I of course didn't score a point and left with several bruises but I did enjoy the cold beer at the Glacier Bar after our humiliating loss!

The second game was no different in the outcome but we were proud to have been the team that made the tournament possible and successful!

POINTS TO PONDER

Must you wake down before you can wake up?

PART II

THE ROADS OF ADULTHOOD

CHAPTER 8
CARS, BOATS, HOGS, AND ROADS

Life and Adventure

I went back to work for Hugh moving dirt, then Uncle Benny died. Needless to say I was devastated so I took time off to help Elsie with their newborn son Mike and run to the airport in Billings to pick up Benny's relatives. After the funeral and several trips back to the airport I returned to work.

This work left me all alone every day and I was struggling with the loss of Benny and my loneliness so I quit.

Donny and I then went to work for Ed Livingston rough necking on his drilling rig. Ed had graduated two years ahead of us and had lost his dad so he was running the drilling company. We worked there until early spring when Ed momentarily ran out of work.

I went to work on a pulling unit in the Cat Creek oil field for George Carrel as a grunt and Donny joined the army. I worked there about three months but I was missing running equipment so I quit that job.

Road Construction

Walling Construction had a road job east from Roy so I went there to see if I could get on. They didn't have any openings but I just hung around and was available every morning. Finally the stake jumper didn't show up for work so I was hired for that job. I wasn't exactly thrilled but hey I needed some income and it was a start. The guy running the finish blade was an OLD hand and quite crotchety so we set out in third gear and went for probably two miles one way.

He was not the hand he thought he was as he would leave a couple tenths above the bluetops or hit them and jerk them out so I'd have to drive them back in as well as the guard lath so no way I could get to the next bluetop by the time he got there in third gear. He would have to stop and wait so he would pump the throttle to show his displeasure. Well noontime came and he got out with his lunch and began to eat. He asked me where my lunch was and I said, "Back at camp where we started." He said, "You'll learn to keep it with you," as he continued eating and never offered me a crumb. (More continuing education!)

Fortunately that only lasted one day and the next day they put me on an old 2U D8 Caterpillar with cable dozer. Perfect, as it was almost identical to the D7 I learned on so I knew all about how to start it and operate it. They were impressed enough to keep me on. This was wonderful, doing what I loved and plenty of cohorts to visit and associate with.

There came a time however that wasn't so much fun. The crawler that was pulling the sheep foot roller broke down so they came and got me and my dozer. I had to pull the roller and that was probably the most boring job I had to that point anyway. It was simply back and forth on the fill and my tracks were covered almost instantly. It was worse than summer fallowing as you couldn't even see what you had accomplished. One day after lunch we were sitting around chatting (some lying going on as well) and the water truck driver offered me a chew of Copenhagen. I accepted and wow it had an effect, in no time it was quitting time. The next day he offered again, oh yeah! The next day I had to ask him for a chew and he said, "You're making as much money as I am so buy your own." The roller job only lasted about a week but the snoose job lasted a little over 30 years!

In the spring of 1992, when I was a Fergus County commissioner, we got a call from the road supervisor that we were about to lose a bridge across Wolf Creek north of Denton and I would ride along with him to assess the situation. I did and when we got there I got out of the pickup and took out my snoose can for a chew. Lo and behold it was empty. Suddenly the bridge was no longer the top priority for me; instead it was how soon can we get back to Denton to buy some snoose. On the way back I began getting very angry with myself for being a slave to something as trivial as a chew. When we got to Denton I bought a can of Copenhagen, opened it and smelled it, but never took a chew, ever again. Everyone knew I chewed so they would bum a chew. I carried the can until I had given it all away and never bought another. However it took a full year to get over the habit. I had never mowed the lawn without taking a chew first. Never shoveled the walk without, never fed hay, etc., etc. I had to go through a year of automatically reaching for my pocket (which was empty) each time I started a project.

That Roy job ended in mid-November when we froze out. I went home to Grandpa Petersen's for the winter but when I got there I was told there was a contractor working on the road up the river from Mosby so I drove up there to inquire about employment. There was a D6 sitting there with a hydraulic dozer and no operator. The boss asked if I could run it. I told him yes and he said, "Show me," so I hopped on. I had not come fully prepared for that quick of a response for work so I went without lunch (again) that day but I stayed on with that contractor, Wickens Brothers, for twenty-one years until they sold out in May of 1982.

That was a very rewarding career as they treated me well and I tried to give them an honest day's work for what I considered a very generous wage. It was almost three dollars an hour. I was given ample opportunities to learn how to operate many different pieces of equipment. In the first five years I had run both cable and hydraulic scrapers, end loaders, traxcavators, motor graders, D8s with dozers, D9 caterpillar push cats and rippers and backhoes. In less than four years I was running a finish blade blue topping the dirt grade in preparation for gravel.

Hogs

In 1962 we were doing a road job south of Grass Range and I had my old homemade camper parked on the Pac Meaders ranch. Alice Meaders was raising hogs in the "wild" if you will, no hog pen just running loose down the creek. There were so many that they were getting into the neighbors hay fields and rooting them up which was, of course, upsetting the neighbors. She asked if I would be interested in investing in some weaner pigs. Well I can't for the life of me now figure out why it was such a good idea at the time. My folks had moved in 1958 to a place on the Musselshell River so the old homestead buildings were not being used and that included an empty hog pen with no water source and no feeders and a deteriorating fence. What could possibly go wrong? Somehow all these "amenities" made this a real opportunity. Brother Larry had the place leased so he would go by there on a very irregular basis so all should be well! Or not! He had a tank on wheels so I figured that should last a week at a time if properly rationed with no one to do the rationing in a rational and timely manner. I got a used self feeder and some grain and was in the hog bidnuss!

Well thanks to Larry things went pretty well for three or four months until the hogs got a hole rooted under the fence. They scattered far and wide. Reports were coming in of hog sightings from near and far. This was generating consternation on my and many others' parts so we needed a plan.

We set up a bait station outside the hog pen as they were not going into the feeder inside. The bait started disappearing and the hogs were big enough to butcher so we hid out by the old grainery nearby.

Larry was an excellent marksman and had a good 22 rifle so he was to be the executioner. A few showed up and Larry took aim on the nearest one for a deadly head shot. Just as he squeezed off the round the target's head suddenly rose up and he shot the one next to it right in the middle of the bacon! It began squealing profusely so the others started squealing as well and down the coulee they went. This slowed down the expected harvesttime considerably but with enough time and perseverance I think we got them all. I'd hate to think I am responsible for any of the feral hogs being discussed today. We even got the one with the little hole in the bacon which didn't do much damage at all. I can see now how young and stupid I was. I did outgrow the young part!

Lack of Military Service

The summer of 1963 I tried to enlist with the Army National Guard without success so I tried the Air National Guard. No success there either. That fall we were working out of Ekalaka, Montana. I was running a scraper on the east side of Conger Hill when our boss stopped me and told me of the assassination of President Kennedy.

The claim is, "You'll always remember where you were and what you were doing when he was assassinated," and it sure is true with me.

Later that month I received my draft notice for the army so I told my boss I would not likely be able to be back in the spring. He was a navy vet so he congratulated me and assured me I would be welcome back whenever possible. I took the bus ride to Butte for my physical right after Christmas. They rejected me due to my severely ingrown toenails (each of which had already been operated on) and my history of colitis. I was very disappointed at the time but could understand their reasoning. I was rated 4Y though rather than 4F so I could be recalled for some duties if needed. That never happened so I am not a veteran.

My First New Car

In 1963 I was making good money and needed dependable transportation so I ordered a new Pontiac from Anderson Pontiac in Lewistown at a cost of $2,600. It was a baby blue Catalina two door hardtop with a 389 cubic inch V8 engine with three two barreled carburetors called a tri power and a "four on the floor" stick shift transmission. I put the popular, at the time, fender skirts on it and it was a real chick magnet!

It had no trouble turning the back wheels much faster than the car was moving when taking off. The first set of rear tires didn't have many miles in them, and they didn't have much tread on them either (cheap original equipment ya know). After that expensive lesson I learned to let the clutch out much slower and the second set of "good" tires lasted much longer.

My dad co-signed for me so I could get it financed. For that favor I tried to get down to my parents' place and help any time I could. On one of those weekend occasions I was helping him feed bales to the cattle. They were small square bales tied with bailing wire. I was cutting the wires with a hatchet and when I cut one that was particularly condensed one end of the wire jumped up and caught me in the right eye. I didn't realize right away what happened as it felt like I had a foreign matter in it so I rubbed it and continued feeding. However the next time I rubbed it I had blood all over my hand. I didn't realize how an eyeball can bleed. I had blood running down all the way to my coat. Mom put a patch over it and I drove myself to Billings in my chick magnet. I got medication to prevent infection and a patch to wear to help keep it clean. The wire had missed the pupil and just penetrated the white of the eye so it healed just fine and I had no lasting ill effects (thank you, Lord). What a surprise I got the first time I removed the patch. I looked in the mirror and the eyeball was completely black. It looked like a black hole with no eye at all! I could see other things with it but I couldn't see it. Wearing that patch made me much more sympathetic for anyone with only sight in one eye. Depth perception for me was almost nonexistent. Maybe the brain eventually adapts but I wasn't handicapped that long.

I loved that car and ran it for four years. I got married in 1965 (covered elsewhere) and in 1966 I was still playing a little town team basketball with the Winnett team. We were living in Lewistown on S. High Street and I took our young son David with me to Winnett for a ballgame. We got home very late at night and I parked on the street in front of the house. David was asleep so I carried him in. The next morning when I awoke Pac Meaders' car from Grass Range was parked in our driveway and our car was gone. I couldn't find the keys so it was apparent I had left them in the ignition. I told Dana Pac must have been low on gas or having car trouble so borrowed ours. She was very dubious of my prognosis but I suggested we would be getting a call from him soon. By nine o'clock she had a better idea, I was to call Pac, and so I did just to prove I was right.

I got him on the phone and asked him where my car was. He said, "I don't know where your car is and I don't know where mine is either but I have one here from Rosebud." I was able to tell him where his was so he could pick it up whenever he wanted. So after my grilling from the wife I called the cops. A patrolman called back shortly and said they thought they had located my car and would I like to ride along with him to identify it. I did and about thirty-five miles west we came to the Zimmer hill where my car had left the road on the right at the left curve on top. You could see in the pasture where it was taking about fifty foot "steps" and whenever it landed it took off all the grass and some of the dirt then would leap again. The tracks finally took a left turn and came back to the highway where it banked off the very steep slope leaving all four tracks before nose diving into a washout and overturning. The patrolman asked me how fast the car would go. I didn't know if he was setting a trap for a speeding ticket or not but I gambled and said I had run it up to 125 miles per hour. He said he was sure it was doing every bit of that when it left the road to travel that far and still have the speed to stick to the side of the steep slope without tipping over or sliding off. There was some blood in the car but no sign of the driver.

So Pac got his car back and the guy from Rosebud got his but much to my chagrin mine was totaled. They finally caught the thief which was a sixteen year old runaway from the Miles City reform school for boys.

I then ordered a 1967 Pontiac Catalina but had to settle for a dark blue with a 389 and a four barrel carburetor as they no longer made the tri power. Good enough for a family man I guess. That would be the last new car I have bought to date.

The Boat

I got to try waterskiing with some friends with their boat and I loved it so I wanted one of my own. I found a used 16'6" aluminum Starcraft with a 40 horse Evenrude motor for sale from Leon Jacobs's sporting goods in Lewistown. We couldn't get the motor to run so he put a new 50 horse Mercury on it. That would run, I could lift two skiers out of the water at once!

I would invite friends and colleagues along so I had drivers so I could ski. I put many miles on those skis and enjoyed almost all. Exceptions being one time on Lake Francis I had my buddy that introduced me to my wife pulling me. He was a dear friend but very much a prankster. He would try to dump me by getting going real fast then cut the throttle. I would cut sharply one way or the other to stay up until he would gun it again. During one such maneuver he backed off then hit the throttle then quickly backed off again. I didn't expect that so I began to gather the tow rope in coils to keep it tight. He gunned it again so I began to let the coils go one at a time. He then backed off which I again didn't expect so I leaned back pulling the coils over above my head to try to keep tension when he gunned it again. When he did a couple of the coils were wrapped around my neck and it jerked me over. I went down like a rock and he was looking ahead where he was going. The water was clear momentarily then green for a bit then black as I went further and further down. Finally the rope broke (it was actually a very good new nylon rope) and when that happened the boat quit laboring and sped up so he looked back to see what was happening and I was long gone. I couldn't drown as I couldn't breathe but sure could have strangled. I apparently didn't lose consciousness as the water again turned from black to green to clear and I popped out of the water. He had already turned around and was coming back when I reappeared. Thank God for his mercy and for life jackets. We didn't do that so much after that and I never again put the rope over my head, lesson well learned.

Another close encounter with "the boat" was on a beautiful weekend during the summer of 1965 when I loaded up my girlfriend Dana and Donny and his wife and we headed for Fort Peck Lake with the boat. It was a very nice Saturday and we went to the Rock Creek park and boat ramp on the Big Dry Arm of the lake. We had a picnic lunch along so we crossed the Big Dry Arm, probably about a mile or so across and found a nice cove with a good beach. We moored the boat and got out to have our picnic. There was a big bluff next to us on the west side so we couldn't see much sky except right above us. I happened to notice the water suddenly start to rough up. I looked up and could see the leading edge of an ugly thunderstorm cloud so I said load 'em up. We quickly loaded and headed east across the water. Donny was busily putting the full cover on the boat and I was trying to keep us going in the right direction. The wind was howling now and raining so hard I couldn't really see the far shore very well. The waves got so big that each time we crossed one the prop would come out of the water so I had to throttle back to keep from over-revving the motor then full throttle for the next wave because each time we hit the next one it would try to turn us sideways. I tried to act calm for the others benefit because if they would have known how panicked I was they would have probably tried to jump out! We finally got back near the ramp but now what? We had never tried to land and trailer a boat with six foot waves. After many unsuccessful attempts we did get it started onto the trailer. We pulled up a little so the waves wouldn't keep picking it off the trailer and each time a wave hit we got it a little further on. We went on in to the town of Fort Peck and got rooms in the old hotel where I had stayed while building the road we just came in on. Our room had two beds (darn it) and I was given clear directions which was mine!

Another interesting event occurred on Petrolia Lake near Winnett. We were out on a family outing weekend fishing and skiing and picnicking. On one trip out brother Larry was operating the boat and I was on the skis. He took us up the south arm which was quite wide. He was beginning his turn and I loved to slingshot out on the outside. If the turn was right I could actually pass the boat but then the work began as you have to really cut hard with the skis to keep the rope tight until the boat gets ahead of you. So I cut across the wake and splat, down I went. I took the normal gulp of air and readied for the dunking which didn't follow as I hardly got wet! I had hit bare ground in the wake. I got up in ankle-deep water and I could see the boat motor bouncing out of the water. Larry seen me and cut the throttle and the boat come to a screeching halt in six inches of water.

I got up, walked back and got my skis and walked over to the boat. After pinning the motor up I was able to push it out to waist-deep water where we fired up and went skiing again.

The only other mishap I recall with the "boat" was close to home. We took it up to East Fork Dam just around the corner from our house and did some waterskiing. That was when the dam was quite new and the fishermen hadn't gotten the motorboats outlawed yet. It began to rain so I trailered the boat and being that it was raining I didn't secure the back tie downs; I figured I'll just use the front winch to hold it on for the measly half mile trip home. I'll tie it down at home after it quits raining. Well halfway up the hill the winch cogs slipped and dumped the boat out on the gravel road. It turns out that loading a boat from a ground level uphill position is much more work and takes a lot longer in the rain than snapping two simple clips on the back!! Live and learn, right?

We went back to Fort Peck, Dead Man's Basin Dam and several other fun family outings with the boat, but in 1969 I got into the sheep business in a small way with thirty head of ewes. This put much more pressure on my weekend time. In 1971 I went temporarily insane (from which I've never totally recovered) and bought one hundred head of one-hundred-pound ewe lambs and 200 more ewes. I rented pasture and had to fence a 260 acre plot in extremely rough country. I'm sure David would confirm the rough part! Anyway there was no boating time so I eventually tied the boat and trailer to the rafters in the garage to get it out of the way.

In 1985 my dad, who was lonesome without Mom, and me went on a bus field trip to Canada. One of our many stops was a tour of a small Suffolk sheep operation and I was blown away by the quality.

Dana and Charmin and Marlin and I borrowed a friend's van and drove back to Red Deere, Alberta in July and we bought thirty head of registered Suffolk ewe lambs and one buck from Gordon Kure. He said he would deliver them to us. On our return we took a different route back through Alberta so we could stop through Glacier Park and see some relatives there. As it got later and later and darker and darker on the first day I kept promising the family we would find a hotel soon. First time in my life I was wrong. We ended up finding a campsite along the road and we had to sleep in the van. I think they all took turns sleeping so the one awake could harass me about the terrible conditions so I didn't get much deep sleep either.

Gordon did bring the lambs later and in the course of things he seen the boat. He had been looking for a good used boat about that size and would I be interested in selling. We negotiated and came up with a deal where he would bring back six head of buck lambs and trade them for the boat and pull it home with him.

We did very well with the sale of the bucks so we went back the next year with our pickup and stock rack to get another load as we didn't have any big enough for sale yet and wanted to keep our growing clientele happy. When we got there I hardly recognized the boat. He had recovered all the seats with padded colorful vinyl and put new decals on and sanded and polished all the interior wood. It was very attractive, giving me some seller's remorse (not really).

POINTS TO PONDER

Must you blow down before you can blow up?

CHAPTER 9
HOME LIFE

Back to Construction

In the spring of 1964, we had a road reconstruction project to Ledger. It was an extremely wet spring with rain, rain, rain. We weren't getting in a lot of time at work until the Swift Dam on Birch Creek went out. What a disaster that turned out to be. The wall of water was higher than the power lines when it went over Highway 89 taking the bridge with it. There was a woman and her six-year-old son clinging to the floating roof of a house and she said they went right over the power line. There were many lives lost in the first several miles below the dam site before evacuations could be implemented and warnings getting out ahead of it.

In the aftermath they asked for volunteers to search for bodies and/or survivors in the piles of debris left behind. I volunteered but got very fortunate and found no bodies.

This was in June and the flood had closed Route 89 which is one of the main roads to Glacier Park and the governor wanted it reopened by the 4th of July. We had our entire equipment lineup close by and couldn't work on our project so our firm was hired to get the road open. We went from very little work to all the hours we could stand. I personally put in a few twenty-hour days and we did get the road opened by the fourth.

We later also got the contract to reconstruct that section of highway with new bridges and permanent realignment. It was during that job that I got the flu. I was too stubborn and broke to stay home (in the homemade camp trailer) and I was so sick I couldn't even keep water down so I got very dehydrated and so weak I couldn't get out of the grader to puke—just had to gag it out the door. My boss finally sent me to the hospital in Conrad where they put me on IVs and by the second day I was feeling much better. That's when a nurse came in with a pan of water and a wash rag. She wiped my face then moved down and wiped my neck then down and washed my chest and stomach then she handed me the rag and said, "OK now it's your turn," so I took the rag and wiped her face then moved down and wiped her neck and then—and then she took the rag away from me and left. Now what was that all about?

After we froze out in the fall of 1964 I went back to Mosby for the winter. I got a call from a good bachelor friend of mine in December and he needed a favor. He wanted to date this beautiful gal from Lewistown but she wouldn't go out with him (she showed very good judgment) unless he found a date for her friend Dana and they would join them for the date and movie. I conceded and enjoyed the evening. Dana was divorced and when I took her home, I met her two little children, David, three, and Kelly, eleven months.

I didn't have any money so I didn't get back to Lewistown until the next spring when we went to work at Hanover. After I got a paycheck I decided to see if Dana was still around and see if she would date me again. I did and she did so we dated a few times before I moved on to Valier for another road job. She and the kids came up one weekend for a visit and I fell in love with the kids. I wanted them to have a dad presence and I wanted to have a kid presence. This turned out to be a package deal however as I had to take Mom to get the kids! (Lucky me.)

I was working on a job east of Malta in the fall of '65. When we froze out in December I left there on a Friday night after work and drove to Lewistown. I took a shower and loaded up Dana and headed for Idaho. She slept most of the way. We made it to Superior by 4:00 AM and got a motel room. It had two beds, darn it! After four hours sleep, we carried on our elope trip and were married in Coeur D'Alene, Idaho, on December 11, 1965.

For you guys who are planning to marry let me give you a fact. It's okay to be hasty getting to bed that first night but please give some thought to which side of the bed you take. It's an unwritten rule but it is unbreakable and for life. Which side of the bed is "yours" is established the second you hit the bed the first time and will not change in your lifetime!

On our return trip on Sunday a U-joint went out in Lincoln. There was a repair shop there that was open. You don't see that much anymore, but he had the joint and put it in so we got home as planned.

In January '66 we rented an old house on South High Street in Lewistown and moved out of the little apartment Dana had. We stayed there about five months then moved to a much newer rental house on SW Ash Street in Bonanza Hills. I wanted to get into the country where I had always been. We looked at many properties and finally found a forty-acre parcel near Heath that was quite primitive. It had no road, just a set of ruts on the hillside and one building which was a finished basement with a board yard fence. I was ready to buy but Dana was unsure. She thought if the $14,500 asking price was okay then why hadn't someone else bought it? By the time I got her convinced we should, someone else had bought it. I was disappointed but winter was setting in so we stayed put where we were. The next spring we got a call from the seller of the forty acres and were told the buyer couldn't make his payments so did we still want it? Absolutely, so we borrowed Donny's pickup and moved in the first week of June 1967.

Sidebar: this pickup was an old Montana Power pickup painted orange and black and was later restored by a Winnett resident, I think within the last twenty years, and looks new again.

Back to the purchase, the former buyer had put in a large garden so we inherited that and it was a good garden year. I was excited but Dana not so much. She was stuck there with no road and me gone all week and her with a part-time job in town which we needed her to keep at that point for the income.

I borrowed a 631A self propelled scraper from my boss and roaded it up there from Harlowton after work on a Friday. I worked all weekend building a road and adding some gravel then took it back to Harlowton on Sunday eve. That was a great improvement until August when we got a couple inches of rain. The fresh fill and gravel had to go through a curing process and it got very soft so Dana had to use the jeep to get in and out. She was no longer "impressed" with our road!

Our New Home

The basement had a flat roof with a tar paper covering. We began to get leaks and I began patching with more tar. By late the next year ('68) the Sheetrock above the dining room table had had enough and collapsed onto the table. It was obvious that I had to make an improvement to save what we had; besides we were out of buckets so we couldn't catch any more drips.

I found a provider west of Buffalo, Wyoming that was making house logs out of dead standing timber so they wouldn't warp or shrink. I borrowed my father-in-law's 1957 two-ton farm truck and loaded up Donny in Grass Range and headed for Buffalo. We got the logs loaded with the shorter ones in the box then the longer ones on top sticking out over the cab. We got back near Sheridan, Wyoming, and hit an extremely strong headwind. We seen an interstate sign blown down then we began to hear this terrible sounding crash-thump and severe-quivering noise from the truck. We couldn't figure out what was happening until I happened to look in the mirror as it was happening. The wind was picking up the truck box, which was not locked down, and dropping it back down (fortunately) rather than just keeping it going up and either dumping the load or simply tearing the whole box off. We got stopped and found there were no built-in locks so we tied it down to the frame with the tire chains. Whew, so close to disaster, thank you Lord. We had a flat tire somewhere near Lodge Grass but had a spare so we made it home safely.

In February Donny came up and helped me get the first row of logs on the bottom so the corners were square. The next day seventeen neighbors came with hammers. I had things ready and those neighbors put all the walls up that day. Donny showed me how to build the rafters/trusses that evening after everyone else had left so I got them all made by Thursday. Donny came back on Saturday and helped me set them all in place. I worked all night Saturday putting the half inch plywood sheeting on. On Sunday my dad and brothers Larry and Donny came up and we put all the asphalt shingles on in February with a temperature of sixty-eight degrees. What a blessing, thank you again, Lord.

Dana quit her job and became a stay-at-home mom (for awhile) in 1968. In 1969 another little miracle came along on February 9th and we named her Charmin after a popular country western song. Look it up, very pretty song.

In 1971 I was working on a road job north of Belt when I received a frantic call from Dana that she had Charmin in the hospital and her lips and fingers were turning blue from lack of oxygen. I told her to be prepared to leave for Great Falls with Charmin in hand if things didn't improve by the time I got there. I left immediately and was at the hospital in just less than an hour. Thank God I didn't meet a patrolman or cause an accident! And thank God they had her on oxygen and her color was returning so I could breathe again and get a little color back in my white knuckles. She recovered from the pneumonia without lasting damage.

Then in 1972 we had another miracle on May 18 and we named him Marlin after a man I worked with by that name and I liked him and his name so it stuck.

The Oregon Trail

Most of Dana's family had relocated to Hillsboro, Oregon by then, so late that fall we decided to go out to Oregon to visit her folks and siblings. We now had four dependents and very little discretionary cash so I decided we would drive from Heath to Hillsboro, Oregon in one setting so we wouldn't have to rent a room. We prepared the afternoon before our departure packing and fixing sandwiches and other child favorites. We packed the kids and perishables out to the car at 3:30 AM and departed at 4:00 AM. The kids slept well until about

7:00 then Dana fed them and nursed the baby. They rode very well all day with only a couple "disagreements" that required crowd control!

I had decided we should just stick to the interstate so we went to Seattle on I-90 then onto I-5 south. Things deteriorated there as it began raining harder and harder. I couldn't see well so was not making good time. A passenger bus then passed us and he was making good time. I decided this was our trip permit so I began tailing him. I stayed close enough so no one would want to duck in between us. This worked well and we were back making good time and I figured it to be quite safe with the commercial bus driver clearing the road. However suddenly I lost him so I speeded up a bit. My eyeballs were pulling out of my head trying to see the road and find the bus. It wasn't long however before the bus passed us! Obviously he had made a bus stop and I didn't see him exit. So we were back in business but soon I was running low on gas so we exited and found a station nearby and filled up. I then began my search for the interstate. I could not find it, despite my sense of direction being actually quite good. I finally gave up and found the station where we had just refueled and I asked how to get back to the interstate. He pointed in exactly the wrong direction. He lived there, I did not, so I took his word and went what I was sure was the exact opposite of where the road was. Lo and behold the interstate was right where he said it was. It was then I realized that the interstate took a right-hand turn just beyond the exit so we went under the road without knowing which of course put us on the other side unbeknownst to me. This was a costly loss of a half hour and of course we missed the bus! (Pun intended.)

We got into Portland about 11:00 PM and Dana was the GPS as she had been out there one time before. When she said exit I did and within a couple hundred feet she said, "OH NO, not here!" So panic set in quickly but at that hour there was no one coming on the entrance ramp so I cut across the median and back on the interstate. We arrived at her folk's house in Hillsboro just before midnight. We woke the kids up again and had a wonderful weekend.

In 1976 when Charmin was in school and Marlin was four years old Dana went to work for USG (United States Gypsum) in their lab doing quality control. It was a very good job and only a half-mile commute. We had an older neighbor lady who just loved Marlin and she babysat each day as Dana dropped him off on her way to work and picked him up on the way home.

We had a stock dog then that we called Champ. With the kids and Mom and I gone all day he was lonesome and he could hear and see the pickup all the way to Dana's job at USG so he would jump in the back and ride to work with her and sit there all day or if it was too hot he would go under the pickup in the shade. Dana didn't like that so she would give him stern orders to "stay" when she was ready to go, so he would wait till she turned her back to get in then jump in the truck. Once in a while she would get moving before he jumped so he would just follow her to work and jump in there. He knew where she was going so he would take a shortcut across a hay field and be there to greet her when she arrived. I thought he was very loyal and she thought he was a nuisance and embarrassment.

Kids and School

We lived three-tenths of a mile off the gravel county road the whole time our kids were growing up. The school bus stopped at our approach for them to get off and on. Most of the time they walked both ways but occasionally my or Dana's schedule would allow us to take them one way or the other. I recall one time we were sitting at the bus stop looking across the field at the USG hillside and field above. There were several deer grazing in the open field on top when I noticed a pack of five coyotes huddling below the rimrock above the Sheetrock plant. Two of the coyotes took off to the left into the timber. The other three went up over the rimrock and bunched the deer and chased them to the left across the field and pasture. There was an open park in the timber about halfway down the mountain side. Everything was out of sight for a moment or two then the deer came running through the open park area and lo and behold they ran right into the two coyotes that had went that direction. They were able to take down one deer that we seen anyway.

I have wondered ever since how on earth those animals could plan such an exact attack without speaking. I so wish I would have had my present-day camera phone and gotten a video of that precise operation.

I believe it was in 1978 our construction firm was going to bid on a new stretch of interstate near Lodge Grass. This was through an extremely rough set of bluffs with lots of rock showing but you couldn't drive it or walk it, it was so rough. My boss hired a local flight firm to take us there with a helicopter so we could examine the bluffs close up. That afternoon we got back and the pilot landed just outside our yard fence as Marlin and Charmin were walking in from the bus. They stood there in amazement as I got out of the chopper and greeted them. That was a very unusual happening for them and me.

Well the bus schedule fit fine for most of the elementary years for the kids but when high school came the bus schedule didn't fit at all. We spent several years chasing the bus back and forth because it didn't fit either the morning extracurricular activities or the evening or both.

This precipitated the need for more vehicles. We were not flush with extra disposable income at that time so I naturally looked for the least expensive cars I could find. Dependability was important but not crucial as it was just ten miles one way and everyone knew everyone in those days, so if something went wrong they were helped right away. As an extra bonus for me—they were not the best looking cars on the road, so the kids were inclined to drive to town and park their car and ride with a friend in something better looking. Took much less gas and the liability exposure was also much reduced.

I had bought a blue Ford Pinto station wagon for Kelly to drive to school. After her high school graduation she continued to live at home and worked in Lewistown. She left for work one morning before I did and when I got down the road a couple miles here was her car nose down in a deep gulch. I jumped out and skidded down to it. The driver's door was open and she was not around. There was about two inches of blood on the floorboard. I didn't know if it was hers or the deer's. I took off for the hospital. She was in the emergency room laying on stark white sheets and pillowcase.

Some deer had run across the road in front of her so she thought they were gone so she didn't slow down. There was a late comer following behind and when he saw the car he jumped. She caught him with the driver side doorpost cutting it in half. The front half came through the windshield and the force of air blew the back window out allowing the wind to carry the fresh stomach content and blood of the deer all the way through the car painting the headliner full length. Kelly got a load of that green fowl slime and windshield glass. When I got there the pillow case was turning green all around her head and it did not smell good in the room. The doctor came in and said, "I'll be back when you get her cleaned up." They got her cleaned and cleared but she had glass in her eyes so they made arrangements for us to see a specialist in Great Falls. We took her there and they got her right in. We were allowed to observe and I was amazed. He had a blue light that he shined in her eyes and I'm telling you the glass looked just like quality diamonds. Without the light we could see nothing but with it the glass just sparkled. With a steady hand and patience, he was able to pluck all the glass out.

We had worn out our '67 Pontiac by then so I bought a 1975 blue Chevy Vega station wagon for Dana and me. In 1986 I was running for the county commission board so I had built a "Vote for Vern" sign and cut it to mount on the luggage rack on top the car. Big sign, double-sided, so it got lots of attention. The kids wouldn't ride with me if there was any choice; it was "too embarrassing." Then one morning the circumstances, whatever they were, called for Charmin and Marlin to take my car to school. The highway was straight across the valley from our house so we could see traffic coming and going. I was watching out the window after the kids left to make sure they got out of sight without incident. I seen them come around the corner but then they pulled over and stopped and I thought, oh no, what's wrong? I watched as they both jumped out quickly, took the wires off the sign, removed it, and threw it in the back—and off they went. That night when they got home the sign was back in place as if it had been there all day!

POINTS TO PONDER

Must you follow down before you can follow up?

CHAPTER 10
WORK LIFE

Advancing in Construction

In the fall of my sixth year with Wickens Brothers (1967) I had filled out an application to become a highway patrolman but hadn't mailed it yet. Then I was promoted to shift foreman on an interstate road job around Bozeman which turned into job superintendant on the same job when the superintendent moved on to a new contract. With this promotion and indication of their trust in me, I never did mail the aforementioned application. I was in and out of several positions of management over the next few years as need dictated.

I was in management for the next fifteen years until the Wickens brothers wanted to retire and I was able to assist in their auction sale in May of 1982.

We worked almost exclusively in Montana but all over the state. I can list many jobs but not all and not in the proper sequence. As said I started at Flatwillow then went on to Fort Peck, Grass Range South, Fort Peck, Flowing Wells, Ekalaka, Conrad, Valier, Malta, Saco, Harlowton West, Bozeman, Terry, Harlowton South, Rapelja, Havre, Hanover, Valier, Superior, Thompson Falls, Clyde Park, Hardin, Manida Pass near Dillon, Custer, Pompeys Pillar, Colstrip, Forsyth, Miles City, Havre, Denton, Lewistown, Mosby and many more but as you can tell we did cover the state from end to end and top to bottom. The last road job I done for them was a new stretch of I-90 from Springdale east finishing it about Thanksgiving of 1981.

The Pacific Builder magazine which previewed construction projects all over the Northwest US, sent a reporter to this job and they featured it in the magazine with the cover photo no less.

Knowing they were planning to sell in the spring, their crusher superintendent, who was, in my opinion, the best in the state, got a longer-term opportunity so he quit when he was done with the gravel on the Springdale job. Wickens had been awarded a contract to do five gravel maintenance stockpiles in eastern Montana. I was asked to take over the crusher operation to complete this contract. I was about as qualified to be a crusher superintendent as I was to fly jet planes but fortunately the entire well-schooled professional operators all stayed on so we done stockpiles in Glasgow, Redstone, Scobey south, Fort Peck, and Ismay. We didn't get the last one completed as we had too many machinery breakdowns and had to get everything home for repair and ready for the auction so we subbed the balance out.

Of course I have thousands of memories of those years, but I won't bore you with many. Following are a couple of those.

After securing a CDL, I also ran the transport hauling heavy equipment on different occasions. I'll not forget one occasion when we loaded a pull type sheep's foot roller onto a lowboy sideways which made a load about thirteen feet wide. We were up on the highline and I was to haul it down to the north side of the Missouri River and dump it off in the middle of nowhere. They had been awarded a contract to build a reservoir there. Tom Wickens had flown over the area so he drew me a map. This meant I had to cross a Milk River bridge. It was an old narrow bridge with an overhead superstructure. There was a sharp curve on the south end so I couldn't see whether any traffic was coming and I had no flagman and it was definitely going to be "one way traffic" when I entered the bridge. I had no options so I charged in. I hadn't got far when two cars entered the bridge coming toward me. It wasn't at all difficult to intimidate them so they both backed off the bridge and let me pass. This is what I decided ulcers were made of. But I wasn't near done yet.

Tom had explained that I was to jackknife the truck and trailer on a hillside he had indicated on this hand drawn from a memory map with many "abouts" in it. Examples: like about three or four miles past the first gate then there will be two or three more gates along that trail then turn easterly off the old trail and go over two more ridges. Wow, that's clear; I think I've got it. So I got the rig jackknifed on what I hoped was a slope somewhere close enough to where I should have been that he could find it with the airplane. So with the trailer jackknifed with the driver's side downhill I unchained the roller then dropped the clutch so the thing would roll off downhill. It almost worked but the back of the frame hung up on the side of the trailer. I had a jack along so I jacked it up enough to clear then dropped the clutch again and voila, I was free. What a relief as it was Friday evening and being in the middle of nowhere, alone, and the likelihood of no one missing me until Monday, was a very unnerving thought.

Another one is when we were working on a new stretch of I-94. On a Monday morning we were hauling borrow dirt onto a fill and had a disc operator to stir the water into the fill material. It had been wet over the weekend so we didn't have to add water so the disc operator was parked on the far end of the fill. He had apparently had a long weekend. I came by and he was asleep. I woke him up and told him, "I can't have you sleeping here with all the other operators working and you're drawing the same pay as they are, so you have to stay awake and look busy." I suggested getting off and cleaning the mud out of the tracks.

I came by later and he was sound asleep again. I stopped and woke him up and handed him a time card and asked him to fill it out and he could go get some sleep off the job. He asked me when he should come back and I said I would call him if we ever needed him again. He looked a little befuddled then he said, "You're firing me aren't you?" I replied, "Now you're awake."

There were many challenging jobs over the years but if I had to pick the most challenging one I think it would be the contract we got to build six SIDs (Special Improvement Districts) in Miles City. It took two years to complete. There was about 72,000 feet of new curb and gutter to install and let me tell you that involves a LOT of driveways!! And I would also add that most people treasured their independence to come and go at all hours without any inconvenience, parking across the street was way too much to ask for many.

It also was hundreds of gas lines, buried telephone lines, sewer lines, water lines, storm drain lines, manholes, etc. and many if not most were not mapped or located until we would encounter them during excavation so I had all the repairmen on speed dial as it was a daily occurrence to disrupt one or more services which of course was also a disruption to the residents of whom most were not happy and not bashful. We had to excavate a couple feet of the streets to make way for the new gravel subbase so that meant no drainage as the storm drain manholes were high and dry.

Of course anything and everything that wasn't just right seemed to be our fault. An example was when we started excavating a street in the afternoon. The next morning when I got out there a homeowner had the city engineer there and said that we crushed his sewer line the day before and we needed to fix that issue right now!! I had a backhoe operator drop what he was doing and bring the backhoe to find the problem. We uncovered the line, which was six inches and we found it had about a four-inch tree root that had penetrated it and was growing right down the line. That line could not have been functioning hardly at all for a year or two or more but he thought he had found a fall guy to fix it. We did fix it but we got paid for our time and effort.

One week during the summer of '77 our daughter Kelly accompanied me to work as she had a friend, the daughter of another employee, living in the same RV park as us. One night that week we were just setting down to eat supper when it became deathly quiet. I got up and stepped out and it was totally and eerily still but there was a tremendous black cloud roiling toward us from the west/southwest. I went back inside the little camp trailer and told Kelly that I was afraid we were in for a severe hailstorm. She got excited and said, "Oh goody, I've never been in a hailstorm." She had no more than got the words out when there was a big *clunk* on the roof then another then another, then all hell broke loose. The wind hit violently and at once the hail was deafening. Almost instantly the roof vent shattered and big hailstones started bouncing around inside. Kelly had a bear hug on my leg so I just carried her there into the little bathroom hoping that would be a safe harbor. It lasted what seemed like hours but was probably more like fifteen to twenty minutes.

Almost instantly the sun came out and it was a nice evening. There was an immense amount of rain with the storm and we were neither one hungry by then so we swept the hail stones out of the trailer and went out to survey the damage. We got lucky with the pickup parked in front facing the trailer so it deflected some hail from the trailer and a huge limb had dropped, apparently fairly gently, on the cab and hood of the pickup without damage and prevented almost all hail damage from occurring to the pickup.

The SIDs didn't fare so well. The subexcavated streets were standing in up to two feet of water, hail drifts and worst of all tree limbs and leaves. It had hailed almost all trees bare and that amount of debris had plugged most all drains and drainage points. We got around by the underpass of the railroad and it was full of water and there was a car bobbing around in it with just the trunk sticking up out of the water. It broke 246 windows out of the hospital and when the wind speed indicator blew over at the airport in was clocking at eighty-eight miles per hour. Kelly's friend's dad had his trailer parked on the last lot on the west end of the RV park so it had no protection. It had those little plastic "fenders" over the tandem axels and it hailed them off and hailed the hubcaps off the wheels on that side. The whole side of the trailer was beaten so badly the metal siding was warped to the point you could have just pulled it off by hand.

On the northeast side of town there was a house trailer dealer and they had probably fifteen big house trailers parked in a half circle formation facing west. It had hailed all the front windows out and shredded the drapes with some of the shreds hanging out the open holes. A few days later I was by there and they had removed a bunch of dining room furniture and it looked like someone had taken a ball peen hammer and literally beat the veneer table tops completely off.

Needless to say this was a serious project setback and very expensive cleanup.

Back to the Sale

Before the sale Tom Wickens did not want to retire but rather wanted to get back into business. He invited me and Jim Wickens to partner with him in a new company. We did that by putting all our assets up as collateral for bonding purposes. The bonders want to make sure you have all your skin in the game to prevent them from having to bail you out.

We had agreed we would need to get a job quickly so we could buy some equipment at the sale and get revenue flowing quickly. We bid three jobs at the next bid letting. We got two second places and one third so it was a very short-lived new company. We dissolved our new company and went our separate ways.

I still had two children at home so although I had two great job offers as job superintendent for two very well-established and respected companies building roads, I decided that if I had to break in a new boss then I should do it close to home and get to know my family.

I accepted a sales position with a local International/Hesston dealer. I was to get a small monthly wage with the promise of commissions on my sales. This was a drastic adjustment for us with the huge loss of income but we had discussed this and knew what we were in for (or thought we did).

What we couldn't have known was that for the next four years we were to have drought conditions. This environment made machinery sales very challenging for the salesman and the buyer. I got my share of the market but the market was so small it was not very lucrative.

Mother

In the late summer of 1982 my mother was diagnosed with cancer. She was in and out of the hospitals for the duration. Upon her first release after they got several liters of retained fluid removed she felt good for awhile. She had lost a lot of weight (which she always wanted to do, but not in this way) but felt good and looked good. She even attended a Flatwillow dance where she enjoyed herself, especially dancing with Dad.

The good times were not to last long however, as the cancer continued to take its toll. Mom remained strong in heart and wanted to seek a cure. We decided on a cancer center in Seattle for further treatment. Our son David and wife Paulette lived there and offered us a place to stay. After many phone calls to get her records sent from Billings to Seattle I flew out with her. We went in for her first appointment and they had no records so they wouldn't/couldn't do anything. We sat there at David's for almost a week making phone calls and waiting for those records with Mom in tremendous pain. After the records finally came and we got her admitted I had to return home as I was in the new job and had no vacation time coming.

They took good care of her and after many tests they determined she had been misdiagnosed. They concluded she had ovarian cancer which they said would have been very treatable six months ago but at this point there was little to be done but to treat the pain. Dad flew out and brought her home.

When Dad could no longer take care of her at home my little sister Diane and her husband Skip (bless their hearts) took her in and cared for her until she had to be hospitalized again. She was admitted to the Lewistown hospital near where we lived so I could stop every day and see her. I was with her the final morning. I held her hand for awhile but she was not responsive at all except for her labored breathing. When she finally shuddered and quit breathing, I called the nurse but Mom was already gone. My first thought was of the tuck and kiss she had given me that I mentioned earlier that I didn't deserve.

POINTS TO PONDER

Do you have to give down before you can give up?

CHAPTER 11
BECOMING COMMISSIONER

Local Community Infrastructure

In 1985 I was visiting with a neighbor from Forest Grove and he was telling me about the ability of local communities to get firefighting apparatus from the state if they had an organized fire department. I researched this lead and it looked promising so I went to local community members to see if I could get interest in forming a district as we had no fire protection except for the local ranchers with weed sprayers and shovels. There was interest so several of us carried petitions to get signatures and acreages which were both needed to proceed. After a long and arduous session we did get organized and raised enough money and local grants to build a fire hall in 1986 which was another must to get the "free" equipment.

I remained active as the elected chairman of the board of directors until 2010 when I chose not to run for reelection.

Wool Pool

Also in 1986 I was elected as president of the Snowy Mountains Wool Pool. This was an association established in 1959 by local producers to let all central Montana wool producers consolidate their clips to sell in large quantities which drew many buyers to bid on the wool guaranteeing the best price. We worked our way up to 240,000 pounds from about 190 producers from Geyser to Jordan and Zortman to Judith Gap (even two from Terry). The shipping was also much more efficient with full truckloads going straight to the mills or export ports.

I was elected to nineteen more consecutive one year terms and by then had sold our sheep so I chose not to run again.

I had a conflict in 2000 and couldn't attend the SMWP annual meeting so I wrote the following paper and gave it to Vice President Jim Foran to read on my behalf.

Wool Pool: October 2000

Well as we all know it was not a good year for selling wool, but before we hear your story I'd like you to hear mine.

We got the wool off in good shape and paid the shearers a total of $68.00. We finally got the wool "sold" if you can call it that and set a shipping date. Now I have a ranch pickup. You probably all know what a ranch pickup is but in case we have a guest that doesn't let me explain. The ranch pickup is the one that the color of the doors and end gate (if it has one) don't match any other color on the truck. It has no chrome or plastic left on the outside. It has no outside mirrors or any other protrusion outside of the door handles and they're probably indented by now. There's so much stuff on the dashboard you don't know if the defroster works or not; it's much easier to just roll down the window and equalize the temperature than to dig out the defroster. Except for the dog, it's pretty much a one occupant vehicle; that is without a major remodel job, what with the chain saw, high lift jack, old car battery, bucket of staples and other unidentified stuff piled in the cab.

The windshield is made up of a minimum of seventeen different pieces of glass that fit tightly together as long as you don't try to wash it, drive, or stop too fast, and there's not much danger of that with these brakes unless of course you hit something. It has the original windshield wiper blades and when turned on in a rain storm it looks like you're dragging a broom back and forth across the windshield. It makes four miles to the gallon and ten miles to the quart. You balance the tires on the ranch pickup once per year and that is when the frost goes out and you drive back and forth in those ruts to the lambing shed. That mud dries evenly all the way around and when the rims are full they are balanced. Like I said, I have a ranch pickup; my problem is I don't have a town pickup. So here it is the day before shipping and I decide I best take the pickup to town and get the scale loaded so I'm ready early in the morning. One of the grandkids had apparently whacked one of the wheels on the pickup with the hammer and knocked about a two-pound piece of dried gumbo off one wheel so you couldn't get over about thirty miles per hour or that side of the pickup started wanting to leave the ground. Of course you have to guess at the MPH because the speedometer broke at 178,000 miles in 1982.

Anyway halfway to town I have a blowout, aggravating but not a big problem as I put on the spare and proceeded. Get within two blocks of tire shop and have a flat. No more spares so walk to shop, get air tank, and head back. The hole in tire is bigger than hole in hose so can't catch up. Carry tank back. They send truck, get to the shop, tires are ruined. Well what do you got? Here's a set of Goodyears. Whoa! If you think I'm putting a tire on that truck that says "Good Year" you're crazy. I say if you got something in a "next year" we'll talk. He doesn't but he comes up with a set of Kelly's and we've got a set of Kelly's (daughter & son-in-law, and they're good) so I thought they'd be alright. So a couple hundred dollars later I proceed to look for someone with a strong back and weak mind to help me load the scale. Out of all the guys I met that day they were all much too intellectual, so I went home without the scale. I came in early on shipping day and found a director to help load the scale. Then after numerous trips up town for one thing or another (one tank of gas and two quarts of oil later) we had the wool shipped. We loaded the scale and I headed back to town.

Low and behold I had barely got on the highway and I meet a highway patrolman. I wave but the lights start flashing and a U-turn and here we go. I had thought maybe I could outrun her but I quickly thought better and pulled over. The patrol car parked in a driveway right behind me with every light on the darn thing flashing. I leaps out to see if I could help as it looked like there must be a serious emergency. Apparently not! About that time Jim Foran drives by and you've never seen such a smile. It looked like he'd lined the inside of his windshield with two rows of tablet size Chiclets. What a grin! Now we need to see my license; I guess it was in order! So then we have to produce the ranch pickup's pedigree. It too must have passed, I think to her surprise, because the next statement was, "Well, I'm still going to have to give you a twenty-dollar citation for not wearing a seat belt." I'm thinking now just a cotton-picking minute here, you haven't seen that thing.

It hangs right up behind your left ear behind the open window. Why, that thing has more layers of grasshopper juice and dirt and snoose juice and dirt and road oil and grasshopper—well twenty-five years' worth! It is absolutely gross. I mean you don't even glance at it when you get in, you could lose your lunch, it is uuuugly! Now I'd been sacking tags in these clothes and you think I'm going to wrap that thing around me and ruin them completely, likely story! But I'm no fool, I didn't say anything I just wrote a check then I thought I'll just sit here till she leaves so I don't have to hook that damn thing up. I sit and fiddle around putting papers away and faking other busy works. She sits patiently with all those lights flashing crossways in a driveway backing up traffic and I sit and she *sits and I start thinking this isn't good; she's probably thinking up another violation so I close my eyes and take a deep breath and pull that awful thing around and hook it and leave. About two weeks later I get this in the mail. It's from Bertie and it says 2000 Wool Clip, pay to the order of Vern Petersen, $.96 cents. I haven't put a pencil to this yet and I doubt I will as I would probably have to get a second outside job. Well that's my story and I'm sticking to it! Your turn!*

SNOWY MOUNTAINS WOOL POOL, INC.
ROBERTA BROWN
VERNON PETERSON
712 W MAIN
LEWISTOWN, MT 59457

FIRST NATIONAL
BANK OF LEWISTOWN
LEWISTOWN, MT 59457
93-73/929

3147

PAY TO THE ORDER OF Vern Petersen

Zero and 96/100**

Date 10/26'0
$ *******0.96

DOLLARS

Lewistown MT

Memo Wool Sale

Roberta Brown

NOTICE TO APPEAR AND COMPLAINT — MONTANA HIGHWAY PATROL   510 A   059399

I'm sorry I can't be with you tonight but conflict developed with the one outside job I have that I couldn't change. I hope you all take advantage of the short lived but helpful program available till December 31 on buck, lamb, and wool rebates through FSA.

A note of interest—I got a call from a gal in Terry (265 miles away) that was referred to us by Bob Meyers. She and her neighbor want to join our pool. They have three years of fine clean wool they have saved since Bob quit buying. That should make you feel good that you have taken care of your wool and established that kind of reputation. Cheers to you!

You are going to have discussion this evening on the future of our annual meeting. I want to make some suggestions. I think this annual dining tradition we have established is not only relaxing and enjoyable but very valuable to our existence as a pool and our future. This meal is absolutely fabulous and it is at least a $24.95 value, in the most inexpensive of places. We have to guarantee the Bar 19 $300 and the meat is another $160 plus. At $8.00 per person, we need about sixty people to make this work. Let me suggest a solution. This is a once-a-year event. It is an absolutely quality dinner. You all have someone you probably do or if not should take out to dinner. You are now spending at least $20 and more probably $25 to $40 per couple doing just that. Bring them here for $16. An excellent opportunity to expose them to a lamb dinner getting them started buying your product and meeting new people. We could have a limited amount of another entree for those who absolutely wouldn't try lamb. If each of you brought one couple we would be out of the red. Your obligations for dinner out are done for less money and you're promoting lamb. Everyone wins! What do you say, let's try it!

Hauling Lambs

I had built a wooden stock rack for the pickup. It consisted of four pieces: the front, two sides, and a gate in the back. I had a toolbox across the headache rack right behind the cab so the rack was designed to set right behind it and reach to the end of the tailgate which was left down. I would wire the corners together and tie the front two corners to the headache rack above the toolbox with wire to hold it in.

There was a school function of some sort going on a Monday night and the sheep auction was on Tuesdays so I decided to take a load of lambs in on our way. The whole family was going so getting everybody and everything ready in time to unload the lambs and get to the function was becoming a real challenge. I got the rack on and lambs loaded but in my haste I didn't take the extra minute to tie it in. Nothing could go wrong in that short distance, right? We finally got the family loaded as well and off we went. I was hurrying a bit on the road to make up time creating a bit of wind resistance on the rack. Things seemed to be going well until we got to town and as we passed under a street light I looked in the mirror. Oh my, there was a huddle of lambs in the middle of the pickup bed but no stock rack. I figured the lambs would stay huddled until I stopped so I slowed up to make sure I hit the traffic light at First and Main on green. That worked so I then explained the situation to my crew. I said I am not going to stop except very quickly to hit reverse and back up to the dock, then they was to jump out immediately and stand by the pickup bed to keep the lambs from bailing over the side. Amazing enough this worked and the auction employee was standing on the dock in total bewilderment. He said, "I've never seen anyone haul lambs like this before." I casually said, "Oh yeah, it saves time from loading a stock rack." (I didn't tell him we were short three head.)

I thought I was out of the woods then and we went to the school function. On the way home that night I spotted the stock rack where it blew out by Hamilton's dairy and folded up and slid off to the shoulder of the road so I loaded it up. I didn't see any sign of the lambs so I figured they must have lived through the ordeal. So with the evidence all cleaned up I was home free (or so I thought).

Unfortunately for me I was mistaken, as one of my most talkative neighbors had come by and recognized the collapsed stock rack and by the next day the word had spread far and wide.

I stopped the next day and told Mr. Hamilton of my misfortune and got permission from him to look for the lambs. I found the lambs in his pasture up on top the rim rocks a couple days later and they were certainly flighty and lost but looked pretty healthy. I took some panels up there with some pellets and set a trap. I fed them in there for three or four days until they were used to going in there then I sat nearby and when they were all in eating I sprung the trap. I got up there with the pickup with stock rack and hand lifted the lambs and loaded the panels and with that had the whole experience behind me except for the ribbing that lasted several years actually.

I never did try that method of hauling again but I didn't tell the guy at the auction.

Another sheep expedition that my wonderful wife and I had was in a spring snowstorm. We had docked the lambs on Sunday and I got up to go to work on Monday morning to a blinding blizzard. It had blown the sheep to the east corner of the pasture where there were no trees or protection of any kind. Sheep will pile up in a fence corner in these conditions and suffocate each other. The kids were still asleep and I talked my wife into accompanying me to move them to the west side where there was ample protection from the wind and snow. I had a Willies jeep so we hopped in that with a sack of cake (that's animal cake) to entice them to follow. I let Dana out to follow them and make sure none of them lagged behind or give up and turned back. I picked up three lambs that were not dealing well and put them in the passenger seat. All went well for a short way and they began getting discouraged as they faced the wind and snow and found no cake and they stopped. I jumped out with the sack, shook it, and they began to come. I turned to get back into the jeep only to see it departing down the steep hill we were on. I tried to catch it without success so all I could do was watch.

We had a TV antenna on top of the hill with a ladder lead on poles running to the house. The jeep was going between the poles and back again but it was taking direct aim on the house. This is a very long and steep incline it's working with, so the speed is getting ridiculous. There is one cut across the middle of the hill and when the jeep got there it went airborne for a considerable distance but still gaining speed and still zeroed in on the house. The old army 4x4 that I used for plowing snow was parked in the driveway above the house and I kept saying over and over, "Hit the snowplow, hit the snowplow" but it wasn't listening. It went between two posts that I had set to fence out the driveway but hadn't got the wire up yet. It hit the ditch above the driveway and that redirected it to the right where it narrowly missed the snowplow and went through the east boundary fence. It didn't hit a post but it did break every wire except the heavy top wire of the woven wire which wrapped around the left front wheel and cranked the wheel to the left which turned it sharply but it didn't roll over and it came to rest parked neatly in the driveway in front of the car. When I got down there it was still idling.

It had broken both front springs and bent the pulley on the crankshaft which broke the fan belt. The lambs were on the floorboard but not the worse for wear. So the jeep went under the TV line twice and through two fences without hitting a post and parked in the driveway. The sheep, which were now on their own, survived with only minor lamb loss. This was obviously the divine intervention of Gods' grace alone as all I had to do with it was to set up the potential disaster and had no input in the wonderful outcome!

A couple more good outcomes were that I still made it to work on time and my wife didn't leave me! The jeep being disabled may have played a significant role in the latter.

More Changes in Vocation

In the late winter of 1986 in my fourth year of selling, or rather trying to sell, my neighbors talked me into filing for a seat on the Fergus County commission which I did with my boss's blessing. The following is an article from the Lewistown News Argus in March of 1986.

Stretching tax dollars important to candidate Vernon Petersen 3/19/86

Vern Petersen

Vernon "Vern" Petersen of Heath feels getting involved with local government is better than complaining about it.

Petersen has filed as an independent for County Commissioner from District No. 2. He feels that as an independent he can serve the people better "if I don't owe one party or the other something for sponsoring my campaign.

"The two party system is the greatest system on earth. I believe in it whole heartedly," said Petersen. His feelings, however, are that government officials on a small local level, such as county governments and school boards do not need party affliation to serve their purposes.

Petersen also feels the county needs to look at ways of stretching the tax dollars. "We need to get more out of our tax dollars," he said.

One way of stretching the tax dollars is more cooperation between the local governments of Fergus County and Lewistown, he said.

Petersen worked for Wickens Brothers Construction for 21 years, 15 years as job superintendent. His experience with budgets and running an operation efficiently enough to show a profit would help him as a commissioner, he said.

"I would look for efficiency in all operations to the best of my ability," he said.

Recently Petersen was instrumental in helping form the Heath Fire District and is chairman of the board of trustees of the fire district.

Petersen was raised in Garfield and Petroleum Counties and graduated from Winnett High School.

He is married to the former Dana Jackson of Denton. They have four children, David and Kelly who are both married, Charmin who is a junior at Fergus High School and Martin, an eighth grader at the Lewistown Junior High.

Petersen raises registered Suffolk sheep and has a commercial flock of Columbia ewes. He said he has always held a fulltime job as well as running the sheep operation and plans to continue.

He is currently employed as a salesman at AK Equipment. His wife works at U.S. Gypsum.

Petersen is currently president of the Snowy Mountain Wool Pool and belongs to the following organizations: Montana Suffolk Association, National Suffolk Association, Montana Farm Bureau, National Rifle Association, Montana Woolgrowers Association and that groups Preditor Control Committee and is a member of the St. Paul Lutheran Church.

In late June my boss called me on a Saturday which I was expecting as I had a quote on his desk for a proposed tractor deal that he needed to approve. What I didn't expect was the call had nothing to do with the quote but rather I was informed the doors of the dealership would not open up on Monday or anytime thereafter so I was to bring in my company vehicle and leave it and get my paycheck. I asked Dana to follow me in and give me a ride home.

The ride home gave me some time to think and I needed that. When we got home the kid's were legitimately concerned about our welfare and what would I do now? I told them that this morning I was locked into a job with a less than rosy looking future and now I'm free to do anything I think I can so it's a wonderful opportunity. I think that's what they (and I) needed to hear as it seemed to brighten up the whole scenario.

This was another blow to our income but it did free me up to campaign full time.

I had a ton of support with neighbors driving me all over the county meeting the rural folks and going door to door in town. It paid off as in November I squeaked out a narrow victory over an eighteen-year incumbent.

The job wouldn't start until January but I chose not to take temporary employment as I had a lot of meetings and training opportunities in the interim and I wanted to give it my all. The commission job would require a significant amount of travel and getting involved in the state association of counties (MACO), which I had already started, added another element. The legislature only meets every other year and it's the odd years following the even year elections so I was trying to monitor that as well as trying to get my arms around the new job.

We also received notice that United States Gypsum was going to close the Sheetrock plant that had operated just across the valley from us and was Dana's employer. They were a large employer and had been there since the thirties so most everyone in the county had worked there at some point. As an incoming commissioner I got involved with their leadership in trying to get some adverse impact funding considerations from them.

They were generous and left 100,000 dollars to the county which we (the county commission) put into a revolving loan fund to help establish new employers. One company that took advantage of this low interest loan was Hi Heat who moved their small heater manufacturing business from Kansas City to Lewistown. They have been a great success and a large employer (equal to USG in numbers) and continue to this day. I was sworn in on the first Monday in 1987 and I received my first paycheck a month later, which was much less than I was making back in 1982.

1-17-90

Adverse impact money to become loan fund

Fergus County Commissioners have decided to use adverse impact funds left from the closure of the Lewistown U.S. Gypsum plant as a revolving business loan fund.

Commissioner Donna Heggem told the Lewistown City Council of that decision Monday night. Involved is about $120,000, which had grown from $100,000 given to the city and county when U.S. Gypsum closed its local operation several years ago.

The county was designated as administrator of the fund.

Heggem said the business loan fund will have two basic criteria:

– The applicant must be a proven, successful business.

– The business must not be competitive to existing businesses here and should provide new services or products.

"We're working with a company right now that is thinking of relocating in Lewistown, and it will provide about 10 new jobs," Heggem said.

She declined to identify the business. "We plan to make a news release in about 10 days," she said.

"This is just a suggestion – it isn't stamped in ink," Heggem told the council. "But it will allow us to use the money over and over (in a loan situation) rather than spending it with a grant."

Council members indicated approval of the business loan approach and asked how the county made contact with the potential new business.

"Actually we came upon this person through the planning office," Heggem said. She added that the planning office is a good tool for making contacts but said input on other ways of advertising the existence of the fund would be appreciated.

"I'm glad to see the commissioners are trying to bring new money into the county and that it's not going for another shoe shop or a dress shop," said new Lewistown Mayor Lloyd Johnson.

One of the many things I was concerned with was the health care insurance renewal that came in at a seventeen percent increase for a six month period. In August we got the second six month notice with another seventeen percent increase. So in December we asked for an early notice on the February 1988 renewal. It came back with a seventeen percent increase. I suggested to the commission it must be time to find a better way as this amounted to a fifty-one percent increase in one year and we had very few claims.

I was asked to find out what our options might be. I put together a request for proposals which we published. We received several options but the one that interested me the most was from Rick Larson of Computer Claims which was a very young and small TPA (third party administrator) out of Billings.

We ended up putting together a self funding concept with a commercial stop-loss which was much cheaper. We were then the "insurance company" so we could set our contribution level and establish our own benefits coverage. This put the employees in charge of their own destiny. We were able to keep the same contribution (premiums) we had been paying for three years while adding some benefits. In October of 1988 I and four other commissioners from self funded counties put together a proposal for a pool of self funded groups called the Montana Joint Powers Trust. It was adopted by all self funded counties that were using Computer Claims as their TPA. It was then our stop-loss resource and it was covered by a much higher stop-loss commercially which lowered our collective costs considerably. It turned out to be very successful and after three years we had $250,000 in reserves. In 1991 we realized that the county employee pool was aging and with aging comes more health care needs and costs. With this in mind we decided to open the pool to schools to get a younger demographic average. This was successful and the pool is in business to this day. We had an elected governing board of commissioners from participating counties. I was elected to the board every three years until January 2005 when I was out of office and no longer qualified to sit on the board.

Another of my concerns and interest was Montana taxation. It was very complicated and I'm convinced some of that was intentional to keep the taxpayers confused enough to just pay the taxes and let someone else figure it out. This was quite apparent when a constituent explained to you where the money should be spent. If their road needed bladed or graveled, then they would explain that the entire 10,000 dollar tax bill they paid went to roads (not the 500 dollars that actually went there). I did a significant amount of research over the first several years and will discuss this further in my reports on my efforts when I served as president of MACO.

We had one lady in particular that was often displeased with our efforts on the roads she traveled. After she had been in a few times to express her displeasure I went and checked her tax bill. I found that she paid twenty-six dollars in road tax the past year. The next time she stopped in she was explaining how the road crew was squandering her tax dollars with below standard gravel. I told her that she had paid twenty-six dollars in total road taxes and that would not get a motor grader from the shop to that project so if they were squandering tax dollars it had to be someone else's. It was a long time before she returned.

The newspaper article reads:

'I'd have to say I love it . . .'

Petersen enjoying commission role

by BRIAN JUSTICE

Since becoming Fergus County Commissioner at the first of the year, Vern Petersen has enjoyed the position and the challenges he has faced.

"I'd have to say I love it," he said Friday. "I haven't been this challenged and motivated in a long time. It's terrific and there's never a dull moment."

Petersen, an independent candidate, defeated 18-year Republican incumbent Otto Jensen in the November election.

He said just prior to that, if elected, he would "certainly stay actively involved in keeping an eye on state funds to know when they are available because this can make the difference in initiating successful programs."

Although it's been about six weeks since he assumed his position, he has made several trips to Helena to take an active stand on the Legislative issues that would directly affect Fergus County residents.

"I've tried to take a great interest in everything because the Legislature is a short-lived session that you have to live with a long time afterwards," Petersen said.

One bill he has taken a particular interest in is SB10 which will affect prevailing wages.

"That bill, if passed, would be the little Davis-Bacon Act of Montana," he said. "It would specify what wages would be paid for what projects."

Petersen said the Davis-Bacon Act established statewide wages "that weren't applicable in certain areas.

"It doesn't address different criteria of different localities."

Another priority for Petersen is to review and update the county employee sick leave policy.

At this point there have been "no hang-ups" with the policy.

"But my primary concern is achieving equality amongst all employees. You need a policy that treats all equally.

"In the past 10 years policy has become very important. You can open yourself up for liability if employees aren't treated equally."

When Petersen isn't tackling the issues that affect Fergus County, you can find him at his ranch in the Heath area.

He said, since elected, the "situation has been fine at home."

The time required for his new duties are nothing new, he added, because he has worked full-time as superintendent for a major construction company while still maintaining the ranch.

While involved in construction projects, he was away quite a bit of the time. He has lived full-time at the ranch since the spring of 1982 when Wickens Construction sold out.

"This is something I have to offer Fergus County residents," Petersen said. "I can stay at home and use that construction experience and relate it to the position I now hold."

At this point, he is just getting used to the new job and the office surroundings.

Fellow commissioners Bob Phillip and Bud Miller have been helpful in helping him adapt.

"Bud and Bob have been great," he said. "They have treated me terrific and have supported me when I have questions. They have been very helpful to me."

Petersen and his wife, Dana, have four children — daughters Kelly and Charmin and sons David and Marlin.

Marlin and Charmin attend Fergus High School.

Kelly is married to Jeff Brand formerly of Lewistown. He is stationed in the U.S. Air Force and the couple is living in England.

David is in Seattle working as computer programmer for a banking firm.

I was enjoying the challenges of the job but I found myself frustrated much of the time with the inability to get things done quickly. Everything in government seemed to be in slow motion to me.

In my former life I was used to making decisions on the spot and moving on. As a manager in private business, if I had an idea for change in the morning, it was policy in the afternoon.

After some time I figured out the difference between private and public and it made the process much more tolerable. You see in private business I was the boss and was paying people to carry out the duties designated. In government the people are the boss and they are paying me to carry out their business, so when changes are proposed in government it has to be relayed clearly to as many bosses as will listen and we need their feedback as to what may need to be modified or not adopted at all. This all takes time, as well it should, but it makes one look very carefully at the proposed action in detail and passes all info on so you can get buy-in from as many as possible. This makes for a much more peaceful and satisfied society than dictating and forcing change on free people.

Emergency Snow Removal

Another thing that I had observed and pondered for twenty years was the snow removal on the missile roads. They are all county roads as well so when it snowed the county would remove the snow from them. Then in late afternoon the state truck with plow would cruise by with the plow in the air and drive to the missile site and return to town.

This was obviously very inefficient so I decided to see what was behind it all.

What I found was very interesting. The state DOT had a six year renewable contract for "emergency" snow removal with the DOD. They were getting $750,000 over the six years to buy equipment and then when they were called out they got an hourly rate to operate it. They could use the equipment year-round wherever they wanted as long as they responded within twenty-four hours to a request for road openings.

I talked to our commission and was given the green light to investigate further. I called a new commissioner from a neighboring county that I had met and liked. We got a meeting with the people at Malmstrom and discussed the potential of the counties getting the next contract. They could think of several reasons that this may not be a good idea and not many thoughts in favor. We were undeterred and scheduled a meeting with the state DOT. They were much more receptive as they seen it more of an administrative nightmare and a burden on the field personnel as they had plenty of snow removal obligations already. This was encouraging so we got a copy of their contract so we would have a blueprint to work from. We had many more hurdles convincing twenty-seven commissioners from nine counties that this was a doable and worthwhile project. It took countless meetings but after almost a year we had a contract.

This gave the nine counties involved $200,000 the first year and $100,000 the following six years to buy equipment.

We figured out a distribution method using the number of missile sites and the number of missile road miles by county. There are 200 sites in the nine counties and Fergus (our county) has over a quarter of them. We have fifty-one sites and 204 miles of road so our portion came to about $55,000 the first year and about $26,000 the following years. With this stable contract we were able to leverage that money. We traded in four fifteen-year-old graders and got four new ones along with a new loader and backhoe with a guaranteed buyback program so we knew exactly where we were and if something fell through we knew exactly where and for how much we could sell them at any time.

We were able to go from two mechanics to one and our parts bill fell by over fifty percent. Now we could work on roads when it rained instead of working on graders. It also did wonders for the morale of the road crew. That program exists to this day.

County buys four graders, loader, backhoe

The Fergus County Commission Board accepted a bid Dec. 29 from Tractor Equipment Company of Great Falls for four graders, a loader and a back hoe.

Hall-Perry of Billings was the other bidder.

Two of the graders are all-wheel drives (6-wheel), while the other two are the standard tandem drives (4-wheel) which the county currently uses.

The graders cost about $100,000 apiece with the all-wheel drives costing about $6,000 more. The county traded in four 15-year-old tandem-drive graders for $82,000.

The new all-wheel graders, which have been produced by John Deere for 15 years, provide better traction up hills. The county currently has nine graders, which service Lewistown and five outlying districts, Denton, Grass Range, Winifred, Moore and Roy.

Commissioner Vern Petersen said the all-wheel drive graders will enhance the county's capacity for efficient snow-plowing.

"It's a definite advantage – a real improvement," Commissioner Vern Petersen said. "The new graders are more maneuverable up hill."

The county receives $26,000 a year from the Federal Highway Administration for Emergency Snow Removal at the county's missile silos. The money is earmarked to purchase new equipment and upgrade existing equipment.

The county is also paid by the hour when Malmstrom Air Force Base requests snow removal.

Commissioner Bud Miller said the county purchases its snow-removal equipment at a better price than private businesses do.

The commissioners agreed that the county crew, under the supervision of Jerry Holzworth, did a good job during the December snowstorm that dropped 20 inches of snow on Lewistown.

"They did a good job and they are easy to work with," Petersen said. "They respond to requests the best way they can."

"We felt they did a real good job," Commissioner Donna Heggem said.

Roads were the dominant factor in our everyday local business. We had a little over 1,700 miles of dirt and gravel roads, along with 157 bridges scattered over 4,200-plus square miles. The population of about 5,000 rural folks depended on these roads as their lifeline to survival.

To exacerbate the problem, the railroads began abandoning the rural railroads to Denton, Roy, Winifred, and Grass Range and later even Lewistown, which put much more pressure on the road system.

I had the road foreman put together, on a map of the county, the locations of all the available gravel pits and the roads that needed gravel. With this it was easy to see we didn't have the proper equipment for the task at hand. We had all straight dump trucks and of course the needed gravel sections were the furthest from the pits. We invested in belly dump trailers and some good used over the road tractors which made our graveling process much more efficient and productive.

We also began an evaluation of bridge conditions and whether we could replace any with culverts which are much longer lived with little to no maintenance. We got eight of those done during my tenure so when I left we had 149 bridges left which is still a lot of constant maintenance and expense.

Another huge road challenge was a constant questioning of what was a legal county road. The records were kept in cans in the vault by township. So every time a question arose which was at least weekly we had to dig through the records, many of which either didn't exist or in many cases were incomplete.

We had road books but they were not to be trusted as many entries were not verifiable with clear records. We worked on these books the entire eighteen years I was there and had some progress but to this day they are not complete.

As chairman of the MACO transportation committee I pointed out the process of creating a county road which was by petition from the affected parties and was very cumbersome and time-consuming. I suggested we leave that method as is but draft proposed legislation to allow the county commissions to also be able to propose what would be county roads by township. We began that two-year project and did end up with a draft that would allow such after notifying all affected parties and holding hearings in each area.

The bill did become law and was helpful but not the panacea hoped for as consensus was still hard to reach.

POINTS TO PONDER

Must you chop a tree up before you can chop it down?

CHAPTER 12
GOOD IDEAS

The Trip from Hell

In December of 1990 our oldest son David and his fiancée Cheryl decided it was a good idea to get married. My wife decided it was a good idea for us to be there, so about the 20th of December we drove our old 1975 Chevy Vega to Butte and traded it for Charmin's Ford front-wheel drive car. So we and Marlin and Charmin left for Seattle. When we got to Missoula it was blizzarding horribly and they had closed the interstate mountain pass so we got a couple motel rooms. During the night it got terribly cold like twenty-six below zero and the water lines in the motel froze up. When we got up we still had heat but no water.

I accidently discovered that my driver's license had expired and I only had a few days to renew without having to take a new driver's exam. I couldn't clean up or wet my hair so I could comb it so I put on a baseball cap and went to the driver's exam office in Missoula. Things went well there until she asked me to step behind the yellow line and face the camera. She said now remove your cap. I said I can't do that as the hotel water was froze so I couldn't wet and comb my hair. She said, "Either remove your cap or we're done here." Well with no options I removed my cap. She was speechless momentarily then she said you might want to try mashing it down a little. I did to no avail so I have the ugliest driver's license picture on record. Against my better judgment but due to my wife's insistence a photo is included (sorry, looks like I misplaced it!).

Little did I know, the trip from Hades had just begun. The roads were anything but good all the way to Snoqualmie Pass where we encountered numerous delays from slide-offs, wrecker efforts for spinouts, and accidents. When we got near Seattle we took a secondary road to get to son David's apartment. There were cars abandoned in the ditches and even in the middle of the road. There was what I call accordion buses (the ones with a trailer with the enclosed connection to the front bus) jackknifed with parts blocking the road or one wrapped around a power pole all in about a foot of wet snow. Hang on we're just getting started. We got the wedding taken care of, then headed down to Hillsboro for family visits. The snow had pretty much melted but it was cold and we had a slight drizzle of rain. It was freezing as it hit the ground so I put tire chains on the front of Charmin's car. We headed south on I-5 and cars were passing us on a constant basis. I told Dana and the kids that I felt the traffic was not respecting the road conditions at all appropriately. Very shortly after that a car came by us and as she cut back into our lane the rear of her car began passing her. It was a bit like slow motion as she slowly turned to face us. She was not more than about twenty-five feet in front of us facing directly. Her eyes were like saucers as she slid backwards down the interstate. That didn't last long as the car began to slide toward the guardrail where the driver's side rear fender connected with the guardrail and spun her around. It was evident to me that she wasn't physically hurt so I didn't try to stop as that would have simply created another hazard for the traffic. We did have one detour to avoid an accident scene but had enough warning to get off without any wait.

Praise the Lord we made it to Hillsboro without injury and spent a couple days on ice everywhere, but very much enjoying our visits with the relatives. We then headed back on the icy roads with the tire chains still intact. Upon arriving in Butte we got back in our Vega and headed for home with Charmin and Marlin following in her car.

There were some breaks in the intensity of the storm from place to place but for the most part it was just plain ugly. When we got to Harlowton things had deteriorated seriously. We proceeded slowly and I mean slowly to the point of stopping often as we just couldn't see the road or the delineators. At one point I could see some red and orange lights way off in the distance. We were going about two miles per hour and in about five seconds here was a semi bull trailer crossway in the road with the lights on, thank you Lord.

I found I could squeeze around behind the trailer so we passed and I checked the cab and there were no persons there. We finally got to Judith Gap and the bar was open so we stopped in there. I called the sheriff's office in Harlowton to see if they could locate the kids. He said they had closed the road before the kids got there so they were safe in Harlowton.

I asked the bartender if he knew of anywhere we could spend the night. He sent us across the street to an older couple's house. They were so accommodating it was amazing. We visited for some time then went to bed in a spare bedroom and knowing the kids were safe made sleep come easily and quickly.

The next morning the storm was even worse if that was possible. The roads were still closed so we called the motel where the kids were and found that Charmin's car wouldn't start so she had to have it towed to a garage to warm it up.

It was thirteen below zero and at least a thirty mile per hour wind and snowing hard. That afternoon I shoveled my way to the car and borrowed an extension cord and plugged it into the garage power and we spent another night. The next morning the wind had not quit but had died down considerably so the snowplows were running. By about noon they opened the road again so we waited for the kids to get there then we made a run for home.

Grandstands

The old wooden grandstand at the fairgrounds was another dangerous issue.

At eighty-three years old it had become an annual headache trying to put in enough new beams in the right locations to support the dry rot aging structure to safely seat the crowds. It was very concerning especially during rowdy night shows when the crowd starts swaying and stomping to the music. It is also a fire hazard cooking under the wooden structure for the food vendors.

The commission approved putting a bond issue on the ballot for November of the 1990 local election. There were a lot of informational meetings and info printed articles along with radio talk shows to try to educate the public and answer their questions on the importance of replacing the grandstand. After a very intense educational process the bond issue passed overwhelmingly! So we did as little constructive maintenance as possible without sacrificing any safety concerns and held one more fair with it in use. We began immediately on planning the new one. After interviewing three different architectural firms we contracted with a firm out of Billings that had some Lewistown natives as partners in the firm so they had a real sense of ownership in the project. When they got the designs approved by the state we advertised for bids for the construction. A firm from Billings was awarded the contract with the understanding that it would be complete by mid July of '92 for the fair. The contracts came in higher than expected so the county had to cut out some items to either not do at all or the county would do. One of those was the demolition of the old stands.

The next week following the '91 fair I and another commissioner tied on to it with a loader and dozer from the road department and had it flattened in less than five minutes not counting the time it took to get the cables attached in key locations. By week's end what wasn't salvaged (which wasn't a lot) was buried and we were ready to drive piling which was another carve out we kept as we had a pile driver and that got the price down to what we could cover with the bond money.

Construction Reunion

About this time as I was traveling around and seeing lots of construction projects I began wondering whatever happened to many of the old hands I had worked with. This led me to the idea of having a construction workers reunion. I took this idea to two local contractors and they thought it was a good idea so they both put up some seed money. I suggested having it on Labor Day weekend and promote it as an annual event. One of the contractors stated this could develop and rival Sturgis, South Dakota for size of event.

I got posters printed to advertise with and in my travels all over Montana I would swing into towns and communities and put up a poster and leave some for them to distribute around town. There was good enthusiasm everywhere I stopped. I rented the trade center and grounds at the fairgrounds. I went to the DOT in Helena and got big pictures (18"x24") made and framed of five different construction projects. I got them framed and we hung these in the trade center and put tables below them with cards and pencils so the attendees could guess the job location, the contractor, the year built etc. Whoever had the most correct info on the job won the picture. The two local contractors brought in a loader, a backhoe, and a blade. We had contests like picking up a raw egg with the backhoe, move it to another location without breaking it in the shortest amount of time won a prize.

One of our favorite Caterpillar salesmen furnished me with a remote controlled D-10 dozer, a Cat rock truck, an excavator and a 992 Cat end loader so we had indoor competition with those. We had a catered dinner there and a live music dance to follow. We had about 110 present both active and retired workers that first year which we considered a great success. We were excited and thought we were on to something big.

Our enthusiasm began to wane the next summer as we started getting pushback on the Labor Day date. Many wanted that weekend for end of summer family events. That year we had less than half of last year so we didn't break even. We changed the date by a week and scaled back the next year to merely an afternoon of visiting and a dinner with music following. We ended up with fifteen to twenty per year die-hards that enjoyed getting together. We done that for four more years then I did not have the time to organize and some had passed away so I just sorta backed away and it died. Can't win 'em all but the try was very worthwhile.

In the spring of 1992, I filed for reelection as my first term was to expire at the end of the year. The News Argus article follows:

Vern Petersen to seek 2nd term

Vern Petersen has announced he plans to seek a second term as Fergus County commissioner.

Petersen, a Heath-area farmer, said there are still challenges to be met in the job.

Petersen has been a very busy commissioner in his first term, especially in his participation in other groups.

He currently is chairman of the six-county, RC&D Committee, District 6 of the Montana Association of Counties (MACO), Missile Counties Association, MACO Transportation Committee and Heath Fire District.

He also takes part on the National Association of Counties Transportation Steering Committee, and is on a number of other boards, including the Central Montana Foundation, Central Montana Medical Center, Heartland Development Council and New Industries.

He is also president of the Snowy Mountain Wool Pool, an organization of about 190 woolgrowers.

He and his wife, Dana, have four children, all gone from home now.

Petersen said he plans to run as an independent, as he did the first time when he defeated incumbent Otto Jensen for the post.

"I see a lot of challenges, some of which may or may not ever be met," Petersen said.

Among those challenges he sees a need to keep up the level of services with frozen funding levels, establishment of handicap access at the courthouse, completion of the grandstand, graveling of all county roads and dealing with cost-shifting laws from the state and national governments.

Looking back, he said one of the commissioners' best accomplishments was an agreement in which the county conducts snow removal on missile roads.

Petersen also is very satisfied with a national highway funding bill that he lobbied for in Washington D.C. The new bill's provisions are extremely favorable to rural areas.

The result of that process, Petersen said, shows that officials

Vern Petersen
Busy commissioner

on the local level can have an influence even on the national level.

"We can't write a national highway bill but we can go to D.C. and tell them how we feel about it," he said.

"I think what happened shows that. If you approach them right and use some logic, you can make a difference."

Surgery

In the fall of '92 I developed what was diagnosed as lumpy breast. My left breast swelled some and got totally hard in three sections like a little pie cut in three pieces. I had a left breast mastectomy at 7:00 AM in our local hospital. I was released at noon and went to work. A nurse called me the next morning to see how things were going and I said fine now but yesterday afternoon while at work about 3:00 PM I got extremely sleepy. She interrupted me and said "at work" you surely didn't go to work from here did you? Well yes I did, had to be somewhere might as well be getting something done. I was on the hospital board at that time and it was close to election time so I told no one about it just to see if things would remain confidential. I'm happy to report that I never heard a peep about it anywhere so my confidence in confidentiality was reinforced.

Later in 1992, we, the commissioners, were in the office dealing with a local issue and a chain saw fired up right outside our window. A tree had died there and had been taken down leaving the stump which the maintenance guys were about to remove. I had been eye-balling that ugly thing and thinking of ways to use it. I opened the window and asked them to leave the stump and we would take care of it later. Following is a News Argus article showing what developed:

STUMP ART — An ugly stump in front of the Fergus County Courthouse became a beautiful golden eagle recently because of the efforts of (left to right) Lewistown News-Argus general manager Dave Byerly, Norwest Bank-Lewistown president Don Diegel and county commissioner Vern Petersen. Petersen asked for ideas to develop the old stump and the News-Argus and Norwest Bank split the cost of commissioning sculptor Rick Rowley of Great Falls. Rowley created the eagle with a chain saw during the Chokecherry Festival.

I was very accustomed to lots of travel in all previous jobs so whiteouts were common for me in the winter months. I was invited to speak at a MACO function so I led with the following account of whiteouts. While of course somewhat embellished it does pretty much explain in detail how they work.

Whiteouts

A wise man once said you begin a journey of a thousand miles with about a two-hour delay if you're married. You can see how wise I am having only said that once!

Whiteouts are common in the northern tier of the U.S. in the winter months. For those of you smart enough to not live up here during the winter, let me explain whiteouts.

You go out in the morning and everything is the same color, light grey. You can't tell where the ground quits and the sky starts or even if there is any ground. You have to travel so you get the wife loaded up and head out. It's cold and snowing very small and light flakes. The only way you can tell it's snowing is to feel the little droplets on your hand as they melt or see them on a dark colored coat.

Of course you can't see the road but occasionally you'll see a blade of frosted white grass wiggle so you know where the shoulder of the road is. Finally you get to the highway and you only know that because of the mailbox sticking out.

You head down the highway doing twenty-five miles an hour which is way too fast but you're starting to run late as evidenced by the wife being along.

Then it happens, you look in the rearview mirror and all you can see is a huge white grill about two feet behind you then swoosh the truck passes. Now you can't even see the windshield wipers. Finally you start to see the wipers but you realize they are on backwards, and then you realize they are someone else's so you crank the wheel to the right. This maneuver results in the contact of the driver's side contacting the guardrail which seemed a little odd but you proceed on hoping the damage is minor. You glance over and see the wife and just to aggravate you, she is participating in the whiteout.

Now that's another thing, women have this built-in notion that one of the main reasons for being married is to aggravate the husband. This is nothing new it's been going on for a long time; you see Eve didn't really want the apple but she knew Adam did so she ate it just to aggravate him. This phenomenon begins right after the wedding. I figured out that at the wedding everyone hears something different. I, the groom, hear the minister say to me, "Do you take this woman to have sex with for the rest of your life?" Of course, I mean yea right away, I mean absolutely, I mean sure, I mean yes, I do!

He looks to the bride and she hears, "Do you take this man to aggravate for the rest of his life?" She calmly says, "I do."

The congregation hears something entirely different about getting rich and getting sick and going broke.

So, as soon as the wedding is over it begins. She makes you stand in line and greet people you've never met and some you don't want to meet again then on to the reception. After a long boring spell you whisper to your bride that "we probably better be getting along to the motel before they give our room away." She responds that we've only been here for three minutes. That's what I said we've been here a long time. She responds "settle down" we haven't even opened the seventeen toasters or cut the cake yet. And then it's "oh look there's Aunt Mable" come on you need to meet her. I'll introduce you then I'll go say hi to Uncle Harry. Yes dear, then yak yak yak yak. Very aggravating!

So, back to the whiteout, I look over and I can see the sleeves of her dress flailing away at the dash but no sign of her. She did finally get a little color back in her hands and face but her hair never did recover.

Soon she says, "Oh look there's a mailbox like the neighbors" followed by, "Oh and there's one just like ours." Now is the time to say you have to relieve yourself. You pull off on what you hope is an approach, get out, get back in and back out the opposite way. When she comments on the mailbox similarities again just give her the old "Oh for Pete's sake look" and say, "You pointed out a couple just like them on my side a little bit ago!" The moral of the story here is when you come out of a whiteout make sure you're still going toward your destination!

In the winter the trucks in Montana travel at an average speed of eighty miles an hour on the level and ten miles an hour on the hills. That's why they sand the hills in the winter so the trucks don't slide out of control when they slam on their brakes at the bottom of the hill where the solid yellow line starts. Depending on the temperature trucks either put out the traditional whiteout when it's cold or a brownout when it warms a little. The brownout is about the color and consistency of a good calf scour except it contains rocks up to about three-quarter inch. So you must follow them up the hill and upon topping the grade you peek to pass but there's a truck coming up the hill on the other side with a string of cars behind that you can't see the end of. You will never know when the line has passed as you will have turned on your wipers and smeared shut the last little peephole you had to see through. Now, in a situation like this, I recommend putting your wipers on high because every so often, for no known reason, the wipers will cut a perfectly clear quarter inch wide streak across the windshield but with the wipers on high you can smear it shut again before you can see where you are.

I want to relay to you an extremely satisfying experience the wife and I had. After so many times being victims of those trucks and knowing the satisfaction the drivers get out of inflicting the terror on unsuspecting drivers we finally got our revenge.

It happened at night in a snowstorm while we were traveling to a MACO function. We came upon a truck doing the traditional ten mile an hour trick going up a mountain pass. The truck driver must have been tired because he forgot he was on the interstate so all I had to do was change lanes. As I did the car pulled to the left quite severely and as I got over it pulled to the right. I realized then that the snowplow had plowed the passing lane slowly so as not to throw snow on the passing cars in the driving lane and that left a good windrow of snow. I noticed when I put the right wheel in the windrow it put out a tremendous spray of snow into the driving lane. I played with the speed a bit and figured out how fast to go to put the spray at truck windshield height then I proceeded to pass plastering a foot of snow on the side of the trailer. We then passed the tractor; wham, a foot on the driver's window then in a split second wham, catching the windshield wiper in mid stride a foot of snow on the entire windshield. What total exhilaration, made up for at least twenty whiteouts we had endured.

We were doing a hundred and fourteen miles an hour down the other side when that truck passed us. Holy smokes, this was the granddaddy of them all. It was so thick that Dana would have had to have gotten out and pushed if I hadn't been going so fast. With that much momentum we were able to continue to plow through it.

Well, I had been over that stretch of road many times and had noticed the "W" guardrail was tipping slightly toward the road so I thought with nothing else to see or do we might as well straighten it up a little. So I eased the car over and when the side of the car touched the rail the screech was absolutely deafening. I may have suffered some permanent hearing loss. The only good thing about the screeching was it drowned out the sound of the guardrail grinding on the side of the car. About the time sparks started coming through her door and burning little holes in her nylons we suddenly, through no effort on my part, swapped ends and when my side of the car connected with the guardrail the screeching was no less deafening. I hadn't hit notes that high since my older brother Larry tried to teach me how to shoe a horse in the barn. Larry had a lot of theories in those days and he often used me to check their worthiness. His theory in this case was that a horse wouldn't kick while tied in the barn. He had one of Dad's work horses tied to the stanchion and I was to back up to one of his hind legs and pick up his foot. This was a large horse standing about four feet taller than me. I backed up to his hind leg and when my butt hit his hock he nailed me very Hiiiiiiiiiiigh between the legs. As I sailed through the open barn door I left all the hide off the back of my head on the log above the door and landed in a fresh milk cow pie. I hadn't noticed the loss of hide and hair yet as I hurt so bad in another area. A nearby commissioner was grinning skeptically so I said, "You think I'm making this up don't you?" and he nodded. I said, "Well let me show you one of my scars." I reached down with both hands as if to unbuckle my belt then said, "Oh this one is easier," and I turned around and tipped my head back and brushed my bald spot. This got genuine laughter from all.

Anyway we must have run out of guardrail to straighten as we began loading delineators through the back window then suddenly we tilted to my side and began rolling up fence under the back of the car. Suddenly we stopped and all was quiet except for my outside rearview mirror hanging by the wires and clinking gently on the side of the car. I thought, boy I hope there wasn't a gate in that stretch of fence because someone would probably broadside us now.

I looked over to check on the wife and she didn't look good. Her eyelashes were frozen to her forehead, I think the only thing keeping her eyes in was her glasses and she had a handful of padded dashboard in each hand. I started to scold her, that just because I had scratched up the outside of the car a little that was no reason for her to tear up the interior but then I began to smell what I had done in my seat so I dropped the subject. I don't think she heard me anyway as she seemed a bit stressed out. I found a Stephen King novel on the seat and read her the last chapter which seemed to calm her down a little.

I finally got the car back up on the road and drove slowly as we unrolled the fence down the shoulder of the road then continued on. We pulled in at the first truck stop we came to and I went in and cleaned up and when I was done I washed my hands and we headed out. As we were passing through the parking lot there was a badly snow-covered pink truck facing us and I'm sure it winked as we drove by.

NACO Transportation Committee

The following is a News Argus article of my appointment:

Vern Petersen
Gets national attention

Petersen named to panel

Fergus County Commissioner Vern Petersen has been appointed a member of the National Association of Counties (NACo) Transportation Steering Committee by NACo President D. Michael Stewart.

NACo's 12 steering committees form the policy-making arm of county government. Each committee is composed of 50 to 60 officials who meet during the year to examine issues critical to local government.

Their recommendations on county legislative goals are presented to the nation's county officials at NACo's annual conference. If approved, the recommendations become part of the American County Platform which is the basis of NACo's efforts in representing counties to Congress and the White House.

NACo is the only national organization representing county governments in the United States. Its goals are to improve county government, act as a liaison with other levels of government, serve as the national spokesmen for counties and advance public understanding of the role of counties in our government.

NACo's Salt Lake City, Utah-based President D. Michael Stewart wrote Peterson a personal letter inviting him to join the Steering Committee.

"All county officials will benefit from hearing your unique regional perspective on the issues discussed in the Steering Committee," Stewart wrote.

Petersen, who is in his first term as Fergus County Commissioner, was elated about the appointment.

"I wanted to get involved with NACo so that the roads and transportation issues that hit us here in Fergus County and Montana will not be overlooked. Many times, other states and areas dominate the transportation and road issues because of their size and population.

"Hopefully, I can voice a strong opinion for our state and our area," he said.

Petersen will be asked to attend NACo meetings around the United States. The cost of his travel and expenses will be picked up by NACo.

"The threat that Montana possibly losing federal aid helped me to take this position," he said. "I don't want to see any aid cut, and this appointment will help to get the voice of Montana out to the federal government on why this shouldn't happen.

"I feel that we need to understand the urban problems of transportation and roads before we can come to a compromise. Hopefully, I can help in understanding that need."

Petersen was appointed to the post near the end of August. He is waiting to hear from NACo on the time and place for his first meeting with the Steering Committee.

Federal Highway Funding

In the fall 1989 I got involved in the federal highway funding reauthorization act with Senator Max Baucus. I testified before the Senate Environment and Public Works committee hearing in Lewistown. I took the concerns I had and some others that were raised to the Montana Association of Counties. The director shared my concerns but said they had no transportation committee. He took a proposal of creating one to his board of directors and they established a committee and I served as the chairman for the next fifteen years. That was a very demanding endeavor but I learned a lot and enjoyed it very much.

Petersen testifies to need for good rural road funding

Fergus County, with an area of more than 4,200 square miles, has almost 2,000 miles of county roads to maintain.

How would Senator Max Baucus' Transportation Improvement Act of 1991 measure help in this locally and in improving the nation's economy?

What are the local problems?

Fergus County Commissioner Vern Petersen testified on this recently when the Senator held a hearing in Billings as follows:

by Vern Petersen

I am serving as Montana Association of Counties Transportation Committee Chairman this year so I'm aware of some of the other counties problems.

Counties contend with different circumstances such as reservations, high volume tourist traffic to National Parks etc., but one common problem to all is inadequate funding.

I'm also serving on the National Association of Counties Transportation Steering Committee. This position has brought to my attention the concerns of counties in other states such as the air pollution from traffic congestion and mass transit issues.

I also serve as a County Commissioner and in that capacity, I deal daily with the task of trying to provide adequate roads so my constituents can make a living.

I also must deal daily with the frustrations of inadequate funding to provide these roads. Fergus County is large geographically – over 4,200 square miles and we have almost 2,000 miles of County Road to maintain in order to service that area.

Also, along those miles of road are 157 bridges for the County to maintain plus another 25 designated as "off road" bridges.

Funding

The funding for these roads and bridges come primarily from gas tax and property taxes. The property tax base is eroded by the fact that we have over 1/2 million acres of federally owned land within the County.

These lands also require public access. The payment in lieu of taxes we receive for those lands has not been adjusted for inflation since its inception in 1976.

We have an increasing demand on our roads contributable to many causes including over 200 miles of county roads serving 51 minuteman missile installations within Fergus County. Most of this traffic does not even contribute gas tax.

There are also three gold mines that ship product by truck.

Due to the loss of railroad spur lines and even mainlines, Montana

(continued on page 3)

Petersen...

Petersen...

(continued from page 1

has lost over 1,200 miles of railroad line. One hundred and forty-five miles of line were lost in Fergus County alone.

This adds a tremendous burden to roads.

We have a water bottling business that ships entirely by truck to many other states.

There will soon be a pipeline constructed by Altamont that will deliver natural gas to as far away as California. This line will be built and maintained by using highways and county roads.

Wheat and Cattle

Fergus County with all that is still by and large an agricultural producing county. We ranch second in the state and sixth in the nation in barley production.

Also, Fergus County is fourth in Montana and seventeenth in the nation in winter wheat production.

have different problems so the locals would have the flexibility to solve those problems.

Climate

Another point we need to consider is the very creative and legitimate proposal for a bonus system for climate. The proposal seems to give credit for extensive periods of heat or cold. I agree that both are cause of deterioration of roads, but in my opinion, a much worse condition is extreme and rapid change in temperature.

I remember when my mother kept the weather date in Petroleum County. I couldn't locate the newspaper article, but in the lat 70's she recorded a reading of -49 degrees on a Saturday night in February, at the end of a long cold spell.

The following Tuesday, the thermometer hit +68 degrees.

That is a change of 117 degrees in about 60 hours. The highways, even though it was warm, were completely white and slick with frost most of that day.

Somehow we need to be able to recognize and deal fairly with this in the bonus formula.

I would like to commend you on this excellent proposal and let you know that the Montana Association of Counties (MACO) Transportation Committee supports this legislative concept.

However, we would encourage you to please consider incorporating our proposals and concerns.

All of this must be trucked on county roads and highways.

I am also serving as Chairman of a six county Resource Conservation and Development (RC and D) Council. This RC and D area was very recently designated for federal funding. One of the primary goals of this federal effort is Rural Economic Development.

I must tell you that if we don't improve and maintain our roads, this is a poor investment of funds.

I would like now to talk about the proposed legislation.

Let's first consider that the Highways and National Significance Routes represent 24 percent of our roads. If we use this as a rational approach then it would seem obvious that 76 percent of the federal aid except interstate should be discretionary.

That could be one approach. However I believe an arbitrary approach would make even more sense as it would take less administration costs in not tracking and recording percentages on the latter suggestions.

Why not keep it simple with 100 percent flexibility?

We have this map that is colored by the Federal Highway Administration. They like it because they made it.

So let us just say "fine, we'll maintain those roads to your standards, but all funds are discretionary except interstate highways.

"I believe you should go so far as to let it be discretionary from highways to mass transit but not for operation costs of those systems."

It probably wouldn't be wise to allow discretion the other way because of the pollution problems it would create.

It seems to me that all states would support this because most

---

Petersen heads to D.C. conference

Fergus County Commissioner Vern Petersen will be heading to Washington, D.C. with more than 2,000 county officials from across the United States next week.

Petersen will be in the capitol attending the National Association of Counties' (NACo) Legislative Conference, held at the Washington Hilton & Towers on March 16-19.

NACo is the only organization representing county governments in the United States. Its goals are to improve county government, act a liaison with other levels of government, serve as the national spokesmen for the counties and advance public understanding of the role of counties.

Petersen was selected to take part on the NACo Transportation Steering Committee a few months ago and will use the trip to Washington to talk with congressional delegations about several issues.

"I hope to learn more about what the funding and repairing issues of roads in the larger populated states are," he said. "I'm familiar with the rural states and their stand, but I don't really know what where the bigger states stand on the issue.

"We know that one of the differences is that we have too few gas tax payers and they have too many. But I'm interested in learning more about the other issues."

Petersen will sit in on seminars and workshops dealing with several issues including transportation, child care, tax-exempt financing, solid waste, indigent health care and other prevalent areas.

Petersen's first seminar will deal with mass transit on Friday afternoon. He will then head to a Transportation Steering Committee meeting Saturday afternoon and Sunday he will sit in as the transportation representative at the NACo Board of Directors meeting in place of the president, John Witt.

"I am looking forward to the trip to Washington, D.C." Petersen said. "I've never been there before and this will be a new experience for this country boy."

(continued on page 3)

Petersen...

Petersen...

(continued from page 1)

Key leaders in the Congress and administration have been invited to speak at the conference, including Speaker of the House of Representatives Thomas S. Foley (D-Wash.).

Sen. Conrad Burns (D-Mont.), Rep. Ben Erdreich (D-Ala.), Rep. John Coyners, Jr (D-Mich.), United States Trade Representative Carla Hills and Sen. Chuck Robb (D-Va.) are all scheduled to speak at the conference.

Petersen is working on setting up meetings with congressional representatives before and after the conference, hoping to "in a small way, have an impact on the new highway bill, hoping to make sure that the voice of the rural states are not forgotten."

(For more information on the highway bill, see related story)

Petersen is interested in helping to answer questions or concerns of Fergus County residents when talking to congressional representatives.

If you have questions for Petersen to address while in Washington, you can contact him at the Fergus County Commissioners Office at 538-5119.

Petersen is scheduled to leave March 14.

I made fourteen trips to Washington, DC during that time attending the National Association of Counties legislative conferences where I sat on their transportation committee and was vice chair of the highways subcommittee. I was on Capitol Hill lobbying every trip. I met some very powerful and well-known dignitaries including Senate President Trent Lott and House Speaker Newt Gingrich (twice) and I thought he was the smartest man in DC at the time. I also got to go to the old executive office building by the White House where I met

President George H. W. Bush and Vice President Dan Quayle. President Clinton addressed our group one year and Laura Bush a few years later.

One year we were meeting at the Hilton Hotel and there were about 4,200 commissioners eating lunch in the same room. Newt Gingrich was to be the guest speaker. He hadn't shown up yet when the exits were thrown open and school age kids poured in. The organizers had sent people inside the hotel to open all the exit doors and bussed several hundred school kids in to disrupt and protest Newt, claiming he was going to cut the school lunch program and starve the kids. They overran the security detail and poured through around all the tables. I just ignored them and kept eating my lunch so one very obese kid leaned over my shoulder and said "pig." I just kept eating as they then took over the stage and started ranting on the microphone. The hotel staff was wise enough to unplug the power and asked us to quietly leave the room which we did without incident. It turns out Newt's plane had a flat tire in Atlanta and he had to change planes making (allowing) him to miss the whole charade. Also with very little research we found there were no cuts to the present funding proposed but the cut proposed was to the ridiculous increase that had been asked for. That is DC logic if you can call it that.

Over the years I attended NACO conferences in many major cities. Examples are Salt Lake, Denver, Houston, San Antonio, Las Vegas, Portland, Baltimore, Atlanta, Chicago (three times), New Orleans, Philadelphia, Minneapolis, Milwaukee, and Charlotte.

I also went to Dallas-Fort Worth twice when we were working on the new highway funding bill called ICETEA. Our president of NACO at the time, Randy Johnson, was commissioner in Tarrant County, so he held brainstorming sessions and updates in his county as things progressed on the proposed bill.

I was on fifteen different boards and commissions each year while serving as commissioner and many led to needed travel. I went to Boston as a South Central Montana mental health board member. I went to Nashville representing the hospital board, and also went to Memphis representing the Central Montana RCD board. I went to Rochester, Minnesota as a board member of JPT as a guest of Mayo Clinic and a contractor of the JPT. We had a dinner one evening in the former home of one of the Mayo brothers.

I was also on several MACO boards. As mentioned I was chairman of the transportation committee and after being elected to second vice president in 1992 and going through the chairs I served as president during 95/96.

POINTS TO PONDER

Do you have to fall awake before you can fall asleep?

CHAPTER 13
SPEECHES AND LEGISLATION

My Inaugural Speech as 1995 MACO President

I was extremely lucky to run unopposed for this position so I didn't reveal a great deal about myself. I thought after this election and in view of the fact I'm now elected and it's too late for you to change your vote that I should reveal some of my past.

I won't give it all to you; I'll just start with the fall when I was four years old. That August when school started I went out to tell my brothers goodbye as they headed out to walk the mile to the first day of school that year. The screen door slammed behind me and I found that I couldn't reach the handle to get back in the house so I followed my brothers to school. Brother Donny had given me my kindergarten at home, teaching me the alphabet and how to count along with Mom helping him teach me to read so I was quite prepared for school. I got pretty good mileage out of telling the teacher that Mom locked me out. The teacher accommodated me with first-grade materials and my brothers shared their lunch with me so I had a wonderful day. That night on the way home I got to thinking and worrying that Mom might be worried and looking for me. That worry was unfounded as she said not a word about my absence. I had to assume by that I was such a perfect child she hadn't missed me! The next morning there was three lunches ready so I went back to school. This went on until the week of Valentine's Day when the county superintendent found me and said I was too young to be there and sent me home. I was devastated and thought Mom would be as well but she basically said get over it.

That spring my folks moved again. That fall just before school started I got lucky and found where they had moved to, it was back to the old homestead. My dad and others had moved a one room tar paper shack with a porch in three miles south of our place to start a school. I was able to start school again at a new school at age five. We would leave our coats and overshoes in the porch on the days we didn't need them in the classroom. We had a young lady in her first year of teaching by the name of Ms. Fox and she had seven different grades to teach in the one room.

I was her only first grader and she had one second grader. I had basically had first grade last year so I was a bit of a problem for her as she couldn't keep me busy. By Christmastime I had completed all the first-grade workbooks and materials she had so when we came back after Christmas she put me in second grade with Donna Mosby. I successfully completed second grade the last half of that school term so I started third grade that fall at age six. This explains how I ended up in high school at twelve years old and I was small for my age.

Being young and small I was afraid of not fitting in so I signed up to play football. Yea I know, but somehow at the time it seemed rational. Please consider I had never seen a football let alone a game if that helps.

I wasn't big enough to be a ninety-eight-pound weakling as I only weighed eighty-eight pounds soaken wet with all my clothes on, that's the only way you showered in high school at twelve years old, is with all your clothes on. I never did get any hair on my chest.

At our football orientation all the "football" players were assembled in the gym by the coach. After a short briefing we went to the locker room, seniors first in line followed by juniors, sophomores, and freshmen. There was a large pile of equipment and uniforms in the middle of the floor. Those big old seniors got first pick and down the line it went to me last. There wasn't much left so I didn't have to sort much like they did, I just took one of each of what I seen the others taking.

The fitting was a bit of a problem for me. If I tucked the jersey in you couldn't see the numbers and if I left it out I couldn't run. Everyone else had knee length pants but mine were ankle length which put some of the built-in protections in cumbersome places. They didn't fit all that bad except they were a little loose around the armpits but as long as I kept my elbows clinched down they would stay up. So I was ready to hit the field.

I don't want to dwell on football but I do want to mention "the play" of that first year. I call it "the play" because it was the only play they ran that year while I was in the game. We were on offense so when we broke the huddle no one went to the right side so I did. I don't remember what the play was now, but that should come as no surprise, as I didn't remember what it was then either.

You see the others had holes in the sides of their helmets over their ears so they could hear the quarterback. Mine had those holes too but mine were down under my jaw on my neck so I couldn't understand him. He sounded like he was trying to shout at us with a mouthful of watermelon without drooling.

Anyway there were six of us and two had gone out to the left then there was the halfback, the quarterback and the wetback. That wasn't really his position; we just called him that because the quarterback drooled on his back all the time.

When they hiked the ball I ventured a bit further out to the right as I didn't want to get in the way and get someone hurt. I then turned around and looked back to see what was happening and lo and behold here comes the football. The crazy quarterback had thrown the ball to me! It was not a perfect pass as there was a defensive guy in the backfield harassing him that had managed to come across unchecked somehow. I suppose someone missed an assignment. The ball was well above the numbers but right in the chest wasn't that bad under those conditions.

Then a small miracle happened, mostly out of self defense, I caught the ball. I then panicked as I had seen what defenses do to the guy with the ball. So, it was decision time, what should I do? I decided to run for my life and took off. I had a fifty-fifty chance of going the right direction and I got lucky. (A friend on the sideline told me later it looked like I was trying to carry a large leather suitcase with no handle). The coach had told us not to worry about what's going on behind you, just concentrate on what's ahead. Well there wasn't anything ahead of me except goalposts so I decided I better look back and see what dangers might exist behind me and when I turned my head everything went black, so I reached up with my free hand and turned my helmet so I could see. Sure enough there was danger lurking.

There was a defender only about thirty yards back and I could see the deadly sneer on his face and could hear him breathing. (I found out later he was a big old ninety-one-pound sophomore with asthma, which explains why I could hear him breathing from that distance.) It was about here where I realized I had worked up a sweat as I could feel it running down my leg. I also realized how much danger I was in so I quickly developed a survival plan. There were these white lines painted across the field so the next one I came to I tripped over it, fell down, and crawled up under my shoulder pads with only part of the football and one wet shoe sticking out. As you can tell it worked out as I'm still here and able to tell about it.

There are two things I never did figure out about that day. Why did the coach put me in and why, after such an outstanding performance, did he take me out?

I was again an observer from the bench. I excelled at that position as well and soon became an advisor to the coach. I would advise him on such things as when I was back with the dry towels or fresh water, etc.

I then said I thought that was enough serious discussion and we could move on to something more fun.

I explained my thoughts on leadership. I said in a board position if you feel the direction is beginning to stray from what you believe to be the right path you must not just go along to get along but rather try to steer the direction back in a slow but deliberate fashion. I suggested they think of it as an interchange on the interstate. You accidently get on the exit ramp and it slowly leads you away from the correct path. But when you're in the lead you should not make square turns. People will lose sight of you and not follow your lead and a square turn could shoot you across the right path and not correct what you were aiming for anyway. It is much better to get on the entrance ramp and slowly merge back onto the right path slowly and gently.

Also if you make the square turn and they don't see it your constituency will advance without you and it will be very difficult for you to get back in the lead as you will have lost their confidence. You certainly don't want to get in that follower position. Can you imagine being invited to speak at a graduation and being introduced as an elected community follower? I think not.

So as your leader this year I will do my best to keep us moving forward in the right direction and I assure you there will be no surprise square turns!

Weight and My Philosophy for Speaking

I have my mom's genes, which meant a constant struggle with weight gain. My brothers both took after my dad and could eat any and all they wanted and remained tall and slender. In 1976 I weighed 242 pounds and my primary physician said I needed to lose weight or risk a heart attack as I had A-fib. I took him seriously and lost seventy-four pounds in the next four months. That didn't last as I very slowly gained that back over several years then added on much more. By 2010 I weighed 349 lbs.

Around that time, I was attending a MACO function in Great Falls and I don't know if it was food poisoning or the flu but I got very ill. I didn't eat for three days and I lost several pounds. I decided that with that great start it was the right time to keep it up. I haven't eaten breakfast or lunch since March 1st, 2010. I limited my calorie intake to between 600 and 800 calories a day. I lost 151 pounds in six months. I felt great and was very satisfied with my new self.

I have remained with the one meal a day regimen and find it very satisfying. It frees up so much time and effort. I was always a heavy breakfast type of guy – you know, sourdoughs with bacon, hash-browns and eggs – but now it's so different. I can cook up 3 pounds of bacon in the morning for Mom and to freeze for her BLT's etc. and not take one bite. But even with one meal a day I have put back on fifty-four pounds in the last twelve years!

So when I was president of MACO, I had to give many addresses and/or speeches, and I was always committed to making people laugh when possible as it got their attention, relaxed them, and kept them listening. As an observer and attendee of many a speech, I realized that humor is a common bond and would bridge the divide of political parties as long as it was self-deprecating. But I also knew that repeating jokes from others was or could be boring depending on how many times you had heard it, so I tried to write original material and recite it not read it.

The following are some of those attempts at humorous speeches. I should also note that I weighed about 320 pounds when I served as president of MACO, so that gave me plenty extra material to work with.

One Such Speech Was about My Wife Shopping for Me…

I want to give you some advice; now if you're built like me, having said that I can see no one here needs this advice but I'm going to give it to you anyway because I'm sure you have a brother-in-law or someone who does need it, you might even be able to sell it to the brother-in-law.

You come home from work, walk in, and the wife has been out shopping for you. She holds up a pair of pants and says, "What do ya think?" You say, "They look a little big and a little short." Now she's holding them up by the waist (I held my thumbs and index fingers together with my arms fully extended to each side) not by the leg (as I released my thumb and finger of my left hand and reached over to my right then opened my right fingers and reached down about a foot to grab the pant cuff and held my arms about a foot apart) so while what you say is true it's a really stupid thing to say as the next thing she'll say is, "Well, try them on."

Don't say another word as you're already in over your head, just grab the pants and take them in the bathroom and lock the door. I say bathroom instead of the bedroom because the commode sits closer to the floor than the bed making it much easier to reach your ankles to roll the pant legs up. But don't just roll them up, roll them under so she won't notice them and if they're not getting too bulky give them an extra half a turn so they look a little short, then you have to button them up. I don't care if you have to lay down on your back across the commode with your head on the floor on one side and your feet on the other but you have to get them buttoned. The top button is optional as she won't see it anyway, then you walk (or waddle) down the hall and, without looking up, she's going to say, "Well?" And you say (in as high and squeaky voice as possible), "Oh they're a little short" and I was going to add "and a little big" but the laughter erupted to where I couldn't be heard so I left it at that.

Staying Alert

I was also chairman of the MACO workers compensation program and the MACO property and casualty trust as well. I attended the national AGRIP conventions each year and one year that was held in Marco Island, Florida. It was mid-November and our convention hotel was right on the Gulf Coast beach. We could walk down to the water during coffee breaks and the temperature was mid-seventies every day with a slight sea breeze and I fell in love with the Gulf of Mexico beach and Florida.

When the convention was over, we had a one-day layover before our flight so a Lewis and Clark County commissioner and his wife and I rented a car and drove down to Key Largo just so we could say we had been in the Keys. On our return trip I was driving and we had a bit of a scare. We had a pickup following us and a truck came up behind him and was honking his horn and tailgating him. The guy in the pickup was signaling for a left turn and I seen him stick his arm out the window and flips off the truck driver. I don't know if that made matters worse or not but after he got turned the truck ran up on our bumper and just stayed there like three to six feet away weaving back and forth. We were coming to an S-curve where the road turned right to cross a railroad track squarely then had a blind left turn and that truck started passing us weaving back and forth and it appeared to me the trailer may whiplash us so I hit the brakes to try to avoid what appeared to be a disaster in the making. It worked and thankfully no one was coming but the truck was all over the road and not just drifting back and forth but violently whipping back and forth. He finally turned off but it scared us and sure kept me awake and alert the rest of the way back.

As president during the 1995 legislative session I spent almost all three months in Helena promoting tax reform (which didn't pass) but getting some good bills through and beating back some that would have been detrimental to counties. I learned several techniques that seemed to be very effective in keeping committee members attentive and effecting their votes. This will be explained later in my Duck Key, Florida address to the Transportation Research Board of the National Academies of Science.

Montana Tax Structure

The two main funding sources for governments in Montana are income taxes and property taxes. This means the second largest "industry" of tourism pays almost nothing. As I mentioned earlier, the taxes are very confusing and the taxpayer does not know what they are "buying" when they pay the taxes. The income tax that funds most of the state government functions with some going to higher education and some redistribution to counties and cities and schools of the centrally assessed businesses like railroads, power companies and utility companies and other odds and ends. The property tax funds most of the local county/city/school costs. This system and its formulas are very complex.

My theory was we should simplify the system while getting the tourists to help our locals with funding which could be done with a sales tax. If we could use the income tax to fund the state and the property tax to fund local governments and the sales tax to fund the schools, then "taxpayers" would know what they were "buying" when they paid one of the taxes. The way it is now the county collects the school taxes then passes them on to the schools, but the county sends the bill so the taxpayer credits the county commission for any increase in the tax bill. Many times in my visits with constituents I would inquire as to how they voted on the last school bond issue which when passed raised the property tax. Many confirmed they supported it but it was my fault their taxes went up.

Opinion Page
Lewistown News-Argus

Our Opinion

Wacky tax reform idea detracts from serious proposal before the legislature

Wacky ideas to "reform" our tax system are common at this point in a Montana legislative session.

And Tuesday, two legislators pushed a bill that would do away with our property and income taxes and substitute a sales tax of up to 8 percent.

Reps. Wesley Prouse (R-Shepherd) and Rick Jore (R-Ronan) can't seriously believe their concept has a prayer, though they vigorously defended it yesterday.

It is quite unlikely that Montanans, given past efforts to create a more balanced tax system that includes a sales tax, would endorse a sales-tax-only package.

The two legislators also distract from the very serious proposal developed by the Montana Association of Counties (MACO) and endorsed by a number of groups.

It is a carefully crafted tax reform proposal that includes a sales tax and specified reductions in property and income taxes.

Fergus County Commissioner Vern Petersen, MACO past president, is one who has worked hard to explain the proposal to various groups around the state.

Petersen and others, while very aware of the history of sales tax proposals in Montana, believe Montanans will support a sales tax if it is part of a logical and fair reform that increases accountability of government.

The MACO proposal must first get through the legislature and do so without crazy amendments offered by both supporters and sales tax opponents (who want to burden a proposal with enough objectionable aspects to insure its defeat).

We hope the MACO proposal emerges unscathed and is presented to Montana residents for a vote. Whether it passes or not, it would be the best discussion we've had yet about whether and how to reform Montana's tax system.

Designating the tax as I mentioned above would take all that confusion away. With that new concept if the property tax went up you would know exactly who to talk with, either the city government or the county commissioners. Likewise with any sales tax hike, go to the superintendent or the school board and the income tax would be the responsibility of your rep or senator or governor. This proposal would have lowered the property tax bill from between sixty-five to seventy-eight percent with an average of seventy-three percent depending on your district.

The sales tax had been voted down a few years earlier (which in my opinion had not been well thought out so it would have indeed been an added tax without reform) so this proposal met with instant rebuttal (what part of "no" do you not understand) rhetoric. As I mentioned I traveled the whole state presenting the proposal and it was consistently met with you can't just add a tax, you must get rid of the property tax if you want a sales tax.

I rebutted this by explaining that rich out of staters are buying up Montana ranches and other properties by the thousands of acres for private playgrounds but they are paying property taxes. If we eliminate that tax they get a free ride. Who is going to pay for fighting fire (on their land), who's going to pay for the road maintenance and the schools, etc.? You are, as they only show up a few weeks out of the year and they bring their own shells and guns and truck license plate and will pay almost no sales tax.

Also, this would open our land market to even more potential out of state sales of land as any young fireman in New Jersey could finance and buy property here for a retirement sanctuary or just an appreciating investment and not even show up for thirty or more years and pay absolutely nothing. Take it out of production, hurting the local businesses, and creating fire hazards of high grass and noxious weeds.

By this time, especially in stock grower meetings, I would begin to see nodding heads and I'm pretty sure they weren't dozing off!

I was extremely disappointed that we did not get it through the legislature to put it on the ballet, so twenty-five years later we have the same confusing and yet more complicated two tax system. The only exception I'm aware of is the added "local option" tax for local jurisdictions which is indeed an added tax with no reform. Oh well I tried my best. We are now residents of Florida where health insurance is much cheaper than Montana and there is no income tax. It was tough trading my Montana driver's license for a Florida one but from a business standpoint it made good financial sense.

So, after a very busy year as president of MACO traveling all over Montana doing radio call-in shows, newspaper editorial boards, and talks at rural gatherings like stock growers, grain growers, etc., explaining our tax reform proposal—and, as said, almost three months in Helena—I was ready for the annual convention.

My MACO Convention 1996

I was presiding officer at the annual convention in Missoula. The following are some comments from my closing address at the banquet when I turned the gavel over to the incoming president:

Thank all of you for your support and especially your encouragement and flattering comments that I didn't earn but didn't object to. It seems we catch hell that we don't think we deserve and accept it, so it only seems fair to accept praise that we don't deserve, don't you think?!

I have so many to thank that I'm going to go through them quickly but please don't think that I am in any way not sincere.

I want to thank the MACO staff, Gordon, Beverly, Margail, Karen, and recently Jack, Fran, Ray and Greg.

I also want to thank my fellow commissioners Kathie and Bud for carrying the load and want to thank all of you that helped me so much. I can't name everyone but you know who you are and I so appreciate your help. And least but not last __OW__ (I had set up with Dana before the presentation that just after "I don't know how she does it" she was to hold up the cane I had borrowed from Stella Ziegler from under the table for the audience to see). I was looking the other way so was able to say, "I know why she does that but I don't know how she does it."

I went on, "Let me rephrase that dear, last but not least." So thank you to my lovely wife Dana of thirty-one years for her loving support. She works full-time in town and still found time to do my chores and even worked in a couple weddings this summer for our two youngest children. I better quit there or she'll be wanting a raise but would you please thank her for me? (There was thunderous applause).

After I embarrassed you all in front of the governor last night I heard someone ask her if she has to put up with this all the time and she said, "No just on the rare occasions when he's home."

I also want to thank past president Jelenski for handing me a well-oiled smooth running MACO machine and I want to thank incoming President Mathews for volunteering to try to put it back together again!

You see I realize that for most of you it wasn't until I gave my acceptance speech last year what a terrible mistake you had made. I have some good news for you. At my age the year went so fast I didn't get anything done. WHEWWWW! I heard that, and now we have a problem, when this many people exhale all at once it causes a back draft in the AC and that's where Legionnaire's disease comes from!

I'm just kidding, I know nothing about disease and besides it's not your fault. I realize how hard it was for you to hold your breath for an entire year. Anyway you're safe now because I'm out of control. I leaned over toward Dana a little and said she says, "What's new?" What I mean is Mike is now in control therefore I'm out. Dana does have a little trouble at times with the English language. Sometimes worse than others like when I came in very late last night, she couldn't understand a word I said.

We're broke but you all have made us the richest couple in Montana this past year and we are eternally grateful to you for that.

Now I know I have lowered the standards and taken away the prestige of this office. Incidentally, I knew that before you told me John!

But not to fear, let me introduce you to a man that can, with his intelligence, integrity and tenacity restore this office to the lofty levels that Jane had left it.

Here is your new president Mike Mathews, as I handed him the gavel.

That was followed by an extremely noisy and lasting standing ovation during which I took a bow and that increased the applause and extended the ovation. I was red faced and embarrassed so I sat down.

Blowout

During my time as a commissioner, I did a considerable amount of traveling. Dana would accompany me whenever possible. I recall one car trip quite well that she went along. I don't remember where we were going but the function called for us to be "dressed up" so she wore a dress. It was at night so it was dark and raining lightly and the wind was blowing pretty good. As we merrily sped along suddenly the right rear tire failed and down it went. I pulled over and explained the situation to her. Someone would have to hold the brake while the other changed the tire and since I already had my foot on the brake and the flat was on her side it made good sense that she should change it. I wouldn't say she agreed with that but she nevertheless went to work on it.

Well she wasn't as fast as she once was (please don't read anything further into that) so by the time she got the flat removed I had the heater and the radio on and the rain was softly pattering on my window so I dozed off. When that happened my foot relaxed on the brake pedal and the car rolled off the jack. Between the jolt and the explanations (expletives) I woke up. I rolled the back window down to try to understand her directions. Apparently when the brake drum hit the ground it pinned her dress under it so she was stuck there.

Now being as practical as I am there was a simple solution to this. There was nothing in the ditch behind her so all she had to do was lean forward put her arms above her head and back out of the dress. Then jack the car back up and retrieve her dress. Simple right, but oh no, I had caused the problem so I had to fix it.

Fine, I pulled the car into gear and pulled up a couple feet getting the drum off her dress. Man, then we had action; the car went back up *BRRRRR* just like one of those air jacks. The lug nuts went on like she had an air gun. She then put the flat gently into the trunk which dislodged the back seat nearly coming on through. She then put the bumper jack in gently and it did come through the backrest. She got back in the car and gently shut the door which the concussion would have shattered a window but with the hole in the back seat we avoided another casualty.

I looked over and shouldn't have as the brake drum had cut a gash across the front of her dress exposing her knees and they were sort of purple from the cold pavement and they had little rocks embedded in them so they looked like little faces peeking through the newly installed window. They looked very cute but hilarious. Have you ever been in a situation where you can't laugh but you can't not? It comes out as kind of a snort through your nose and sometimes more than a snort comes out.

Well anyway now I see she was mad. For you younger folks I should explain for your future benefit that women have two kinds of mad. There is shouting mad and then there is lock jaw mad and you handle them in VERY different ways. In a shouting mad you say not a single word, you listen!! You must put on a good front; you must look directly at her and nod your head occasionally. Now the nodding will come naturally but you must not let your eyes fall shut. That happened to me one time early on and when I came to I had a scab on the bridge of my nose and both my eyes were black so you must pay attention. Those black eyes were so hard to explain I finally just started saying I had a raccoon somewhere up in my family tree and I was where it re-emerged.

In a lock jaw mad she will not say a word and will not look at you so you must do the talking. The secret is to figure out who she is mad at then start making disparaging remarks about them. She will eventually start agreeing with you and work her way out of the "mad." So in this case I started with the tire manufacturers, they just don't make quality tires like they used to but it wasn't long until I could see they weren't the target of her anger so I started in on old Fred, our tire guy. I commented that he should have been more on the ball. He had only been telling me for about two months, every time I stopped to have him air that tire up, that I needed to put a new one on and two months is not near enough time for a big decision like that and besides he had been wrong for two months. Well it turns out it wasn't old Fred either, so I went after the roofing contractors. After a hail storm they shovel all those old shingles off into their old dump truck then head out on the highway for the landfill with the shingle nails slowly rattling to the bottom and falling out on the highway. It wasn't them either that she was mad at but by then we had arrived at our destination so I'll have to figure that one out later, and I will, being the old pro I am.

NACO Criminal Justice Committee

Jane Jelenski was serving on the NACO criminal justice committee in 95/96 while I was president of MACO and they had a committee meeting in Billings, Montana. Jane asked me to give an opening welcome address to those national members. I headed down to Billings with a suit and tie all tidied in place. I stopped in Roundup and went to the restroom and bought a cup of coffee in a covered Styrofoam cup. It was quite hot so I placed it in the cup holder to cool. Several miles later I took it out and tipped it up to take a slurp. Apparently I had jarred the lid a bit in handling the cup because it popped off and dumped coffee all down one side of my shirt and jacket! No extra time and no extra clothes so keep on trucken. It didn't show on the jacket much but the shirt was brown all the way down the right side.

I went to the head of the big crowded conference table as Jane introduced me.

I thanked her and said good morning to the attendees then I quickly explained that I had decided to stain my shirt brown this morning but after a good start realized I didn't have enough coffee so I only got half done. That turned out to be a good ice breaker, got a good laugh and I was in!

In that era the U of M Missoula Grizzlies was a very dominating football giant. They were in the national playoffs and sometimes the national championship game every year. This meant they beat the MSU Bozeman Bobcats every year. I pointed out that we had a commissioner from both cities present and told the following story.

Eastern Montana Rancher

This story isn't exactly my invention as I had heard a version of it somewhere before concerning a whole different place.

I told them about an eastern Montana student that went to MSU in Bozeman from the ranch and got a degree in ag science then went back and took over the ranch from his folks. He barely got by and the summers got hotter drier and drier hotter and he continued to pray for rain but very little came. He lost his life in an accident and by then had lost his faith so he went to hell. After the first day the devil approached him and asked how he liked the heat. He said, "Oh it's great, it feels just like a good hay drying day in eastern Montana." This upset the devil so the next day he cranked the heat up as high as it would go. He then approached him and asked how he liked it now. He said, "Oh it's great, feels just like a good grain harvest day in eastern Montana," This really upset the devil so he turned the heat completely off. That day when the rancher came out with an icicle hanging from his nose and frosted eyebrows the devil says, "Now what do you think?", and he replied, "I think the Bobcats beat the Grizzlies!"

Long Belt

On another occasion while addressing the Montana road supervisors I told them I envied them as they could just drop their belt, buckle end down, and thread it around their waist. I however had a lot of trouble with that as the pile of belt on the floor when I started threading would act just like jumper cables and tie itself in knots. I finally solved this by buying one of those big old bull rider belt buckles. That worked just like a sinker on a set line so I could cast it down the hall and just reel it in as I threaded it around my waist. Sometimes it would snag on the door frame as it tried to make the corner but I could just flip it loose!

Suspenders

I started another address with the statement that getting dressed was a challenge for me. I asked the assembly if they'd ever tried to dress an egg. I said it's very hard to keep the pants up so I solved that problem with a big pair of black suspenders. I didn't realize just how big they were until this morning in the hotel room. When I woke up I threw the covers back and they formed kind of a triangle which made the sheet open on the whole bed so all was white. I was changing pants so I threw the suspenders on the bed and went to the shower. When I came back here were those suspenders scattered all over the bed. It was startling; instead of looking like I was going to get dressed it looked more like I was getting ready to harness a team!

Another Aggravating Thing

When my wife asks me to do something and I say I will, I'm going to do it. She doesn't have to keep harping about it and reminding me every six months or so!

POINTS TO PONDER

Must you fall up before you can fall down?

CHAPTER 14
MEETINGS

Road Supervisor's Road Trip

At the NACO meetings they always had vendors set up to show and promote their products to the county commissioners. I got acquainted with the rep for 3M Corporation. They make road signs and striping paint. They had come out with a very high intensity reflection for signs and striping paints the same. Of course all the counties have a lot of need for both. The samples were very impressive. I had been going to the Montana road supervisor's conventions every year to report on the NACO transportation committee efforts so I knew them well. In my discussions with the rep about their manufacturing process I also inquired about the possibility of touring the plant. She said they do that so she encouraged me to put it together. MACO's safety director helped me and we chartered a bus to go to Minneapolis. We had nearly forty county reps on the bus. We hit some bad weather and just a few miles west of Bismarck, North Dakota we see a tornado about a quarter mile away. It was grey until it touched down then started turning black from the bottom up. Then another one crossed the highway right behind the bus.

I had a camera hanging around my neck but I just sat there with my mouth open and did not get one picture! We stopped in Bismarck to change bus drivers and there were sirens blaring all around.

The road supervisors had brought along some liquid refreshments for happy hour and by the time we got to Fargo they were running out of supplies so the bus pulled in and was about to stop at a truck stop convenience store when someone spotted Harry's Happy Bottles liquor store across the street. So about forty happy customers strode in. The attendant was just closing up and had shut his computer down so he said we may not be able to buy anything but he would call his boss and see what to do. I was close enough I could hear the boss answer the call. The employee told him of the dilemma and asked for his direction. He said do what you have to do but SELL SELL!! I'm pretty sure he sold more than he had all day so all were happy.

The 3M rep met us at the hotel about midnight where they had rooms reserved and paid for. We toured the plant and had different engineers give us presentations all day. After they served us dinner we went to their private driving test tracks. It was dark by then and we took turns riding around in the vans to observe the signs and markings. They had regular paint striping with the new high intensity striping right beside it. They also made their own rain so when we hit that the dull old paint totally disappeared and the new method shined through the water like it had lights under it. WOW, what a tremendous difference! The signs were much the same, they had a new stop sign with the regular red and white paint and one right beside it with the high resolution coating. It was so bright you had to look real close to even see the regular one.

I am sure 3M got their investment in our weekend visit well covered as the demand for their products increased in Montana and North Dakota. The rep told me later they had to hire another sales rep for those states.

Our bus ride back was much more subdued and uneventful so we didn't have to stop in Fargo.

Roundtable Report

In December of 1997 I was asked to attend a weekend roundtable with Senator Burns at Rock Creek Lodge near Red Lodge to represent MACO. Following is the report I turned in to MACO afterwards.

Senator Burns Roundtable
December 2, 1997

I believe we had a very productive gathering with Senator Burns and his staff. We of course got better acquainted, which never hurts, but more importantly reinforced some concerns that I think they took very seriously and will continue to strive to resolve them at the national level.

I brought up the American Heritage River Act, the ISTEA re-authorization, the underfunded PILT issue, the continued assault on the clean air standards by the administration and the buracuracy could strangle our farmers and local government (with dusty roads) as well as many others., Also, I brought up the Endangered Species Act and its need to be revisited as it has far surpassed any legislative intent and is now violating peoples constitutional rights and in some cases taking peoples private property both real and personal (land and stock) without compensation and even without their ability to protect themselves and their property without prosecution.

I was asked to have MACO submit specifically what changes we want. They do not want to open the ESA Legislation until they know exactly what changes to make and furthermore already have the votes to get it done. They are afraid that without that preparation we could actually lose to other interests and make it worse.

They also want letters from Individual counties sent to Burns, Baucus and Hill opposing the American Heritage Rivers Act. They have MACO's Board decision but want more letters.

Well, thats enough nonsense. Let me get serious for a minute.

I got to my room (very late) and knowing I had to be in Helena by 10 A.M. I called the front desk to ask for a wake up call for 4 A.M. This very cordial young sounding female voice comes on and wants to help. OK, lets see, that'd be 0500 Room 103 push oops! Now lets see here, just a minute then she started talking to someone on another phone without putting me on hold, No you can't come over here---no, I don't get off till 7---No, I have to be home by 8---No, I said I've got to go, Good-bye.

Obviously, her boyfriend has trouble with 2 syllable words like No! I don't want to sound too critical of him though, as I remember when I had that same problem. She was a beautiful and gracious girl but if it were up to her, I still wouldn't know what time it was. But I've broadend all over since then. I now even understand some three syllable words like shut up, no way and go away.

"Now lets see here, you said 5 o'clock? Yes. O.K. 0500. Is this room #203? No, its #103. Oh, Yeah, O.K. Now push enter. There I think we're all set. How reassuring. I'm pretty sure now I won't get the call but little did I know that was the least of my worries. I turned on the lights for the first time and wow!, what a room. It was huge. It had a refrigerator, a microwave oven, a counter top electric range, a sink, a bathroom, a wet bar, stocked (and locked), a kitchen table and 6 chairs, a recliner, a love seat couch, television and end tables and <u>NO</u> bed. Then I discovered a side door and thought wow! a separate bedroom. I tried to open it and a voice from the other side said "knock it off or I'll call security."

At least I knew now how to get help. I finally found a cupboard looking thing that folded down from the wall, a hide-a-bed? It looked narrow but I'm used to king sized. I found a blanket and pillow in the closet, throwed them on the "bed" and laid down. Wow! This "bed" is harder then the back of my head. I only sleep on three sides, left, right and rear. I don't sleep on my stomach for obvious reasons (my balance isn't that good). Anyway, it took about 15 minutes to paralyze a side so about every 45 minutes I would have to get up and rest awhile. Fortunately, I had drunk copious quantities of beer before going to bed so the rest periods weren't entirely a waste of time. I finally gave up and went to the shower. When I got out the phone was ringing and the guy in my bedroom was banging on the side door saying "answer the damn phone or I'm going to call security."

In retrospect, I think they overbooked and had someone in my bedroom and I slept on the ironing board.

Alaska

When Charmin graduated college with her chemical engineering degree she took a job with ARCO in Alaska. In 1994 we flew up to see her and she had an Alaska car trip all planned for us with B&Bs already reserved. We took her car and traveled almost all the paved roads that you can drive to Anchorage. We stopped at Denali National Park and drove in to the end of the road and seen caribou and brown bear. We also could see the entirety of Mt. McKinley clear to the top (so majestic). That was the last day cars were allowed in for the season so the next day we rode the tour bus through the same route, but of course we had a tour guide talking all the way so it was more interesting. We could not see the top half of the mountain as it was clouded in and the guide said that was normal so we then knew how fortunate we had been the previous day.

We went through to Fairbanks and stopped at the town of North Pole where Dana found a Sports Inc member store so we went in and she found one of the employees that she knew from phone discussions. Dana was employed at Sports Inc Corporate office in Lewistown at that time.

We also put the car on a railroad car and went through the tunnel to Whitaker (there was no road to Whitaker at that time). We then put the car on a ferry and set sail for Valdez. They took us up near a glacier where we could see it calving and hear the tremendous splashing when the huge chunks of ice hit the water. We docked at Valdez and drove back to Anchorage. What a wonderful experience.

We were in Alaska in 1998 visiting our daughter Charmin and sightseeing. NACO was meeting in Juneau while we were there so I went in their convention center and visited with several friends and staff I had worked with. Several didn't realize I was no longer a commissioner or member and were accusing me of goofing off instead of attending the committee meetings. Oh well.

Dana also made a third trip by herself after the birth of a grandson in Anchorage and while there got to fly as a guest on an ARCO flight to view the North Slope. This was a once in a lifetime opportunity for her.

National Conference on Transportation Planning: Duck Key, Florida

One day in late April of 2003 I was working at my desk when the phone rang. I was shocked when I answered it and it was the MDOT (Michigan Department of Transportation director) and she wanted to know if I would address the conference on statewide transportation planning in Duck Key, Florida in May. I asked her what she would be looking for. She said they wanted a local elected official to help them understand how to effectively connect with them. I said I would certainly consider it but would like a little more specificity on what they were expecting.

I soon received a packet in the mail with all the details of location and times and thanking me for accepting the invitation! OK, as usual I will just have to wing it. I was busy with several local projects but kept thinking I needed to get something put together for this commitment, but there's plenty of time! Pretty soon it was May but still no spare time. I was chairman of the board for the local HRDC and we had our annual meeting on Friday, May 16th and I felt I had to be there so I was to fly to Miami on Saturday to speak on Sunday. I took a tablet as carry-on and thought with this long flight something will come to me. I just happened to have a very talkative neighbor on the way to Atlanta for a plane change. Oh well I can write it between Atlanta and Miami. Well during that last leg I was worrying about renting a car and trying to find Duck Key, Florida in the middle of the night and realizing finally that I was in over my head. A sheepherder heading to speak to a national audience of PHDs and all kinds of other letters behind their names and a totally blank tablet to go by!

When I got to the rental car desk in Miami there was a well-dressed gentleman with a brief case renting a car. I got bold and asked him if he was going to Duck Key for a conference. He was indeed so I asked him if he wanted some company and he accepted. Whew, dodged another bullet. We had a good ride and visit so at least now I knew someone that would be there. We got there about midnight and most everything was closed. I did get room service to bring me a pathetic packaged sandwich and a six-pack. I was very tired so I went to bed as I would have all morning to write a speech. I was up early and walked to where I was to speak so I would not get lost and be late. I went back to the room and wrote some sort of skeleton notes to remind me of topics to cover.

Conference on Statewide Transportation Planning: *Making Connections*
Duck Key, Florida
May 18-20, 2003

Conference Agenda

Sunday, May 18

11:00 am – 5:00 pm
 Registration *(Flagler Foyer)*

1:00 pm
 Welcome *(Flagler West)*
 Ysela Llort, Florida DOT
 Neil Pederson, Maryland SHA

1:15 – 3:15 pm
 Plenary Session: Making the Connection to the Political Process and Decision-Makers *(Flagler West)*
 Moderator: Susan Mortel, Michigan DOT
 Richard J. Kaplan, Mayor, City of Lauderhill, Florida
 Vern Petersen, Commissioner, Fergus County, Montana
 Gloria Jeff, Director, Michigan DOT

3:15 – 3:30 pm
 Break

3:30 – 5:00 pm
 Breakout Sessions
 Breakout Session 1: Tools, Data, and Technology (Osprey)
 Breakout Session 2: Research (Key Deer)
 Breakout Session 3: Institutional and Policy Direction (Sea Turtle)

5:00 – 6:30 pm
 Reception *(cash bar) (Atlantic Pool Deck)*
 "All American Cookout" (with some Florida specialties)

Page 1 of 4

Statewide Transportation Planning Conference
Transportation Research Board of the
National Academies
Presentation of Vernon Petersen

Ya'll know what to do when scalded with hot water? You drown it instantly with large quantities of ice cold water! I discovered this remedy quite by accident while showering in a convention hotel.

As Mike said, I am from Montana, so I'd better talk briefly about Montana. Perhaps that will help explain the warped views I'm going to give you today.

We are up North a bit (it was 33° when I left the State yesterday morning) and we are very rural. We are a big State, about 600 miles long and almost 400 miles wide with about 900,000 people most of the time. A little less now because I'm down here for the weekend but thereabouts . In my County we have 4300 square miles of turf, about 2000 miles of county roads and about 6000 people outside the County seat to pay for those roads and 157 bridges. Here is a graph, you can't read it but it shows Florida down here with 26% Rural Annual Vehicle Miles of Travel and big old rural Texas here at 33% and here is Montana right at the top with 78%RAVMT.

So after all that it might surprise you to know we have mass transit in Montana. We consider anything over 3 loaded horse trailers in a row to be mass transit.

Anyway like I said we're rural and don't have a lot of budget:
- That means I have no staff;
- I also don't do computers, that means no power point;
- I also don't type, that means I can't read this.

 So please bear with me.

I like the emphasis your planners used for this workshop of "Connecting with the Decision Makers". And certainly that is what it takes. Casual contact will not get the job done.

I hope I have some insights that have been gained through many a year of trial and error on my part.

I am a decision maker of sorts even tho I'm at the bottom of the food chain, so to speak, of decision makers. Nevertheless, I know how I react to many different situations.

So the first thing I want to point out, and I can't over emphasize it, is that all the decision makers are human! Human! Okay, Okay I know there are exceptions but they are rare. But seriously they are human and almost all humans respond well to two things: courtesy and respect.

Think about that for a moment – your Mom was a decision maker. How did she respond to you? Did you get a good result form whining and demanding? What about when you were courteous and respectful. You may not have always gotten what you wanted but I'm betting you got a much more thoughtful and better explained response when you were polite.

Remember the old saying "I Learned all I ever needed to know in Kindergarten"? While that's a bit of an exaggeration, it has a lot of merit.

Now lets talk about the decision makers.

Lets talk about the political side first.

I'd like to touch on 3 levels – local, state and federal.

Local if its open door like ours, stop in, introduce yourself, let them know who you are and what you do. Tell them thanks for serving in a tough job. Remember them and if you see one of them at a function, say "hi" and be sure to identify your self again. Some can remember, most like me can't and will appreciate not having to try to guess who you are, and will likely remember you after that second or third encounter.

If you can't get in easily watch the paper and write a thank you for something you see them do that you agree with. Trust me. They don't get many of these and they will likely remember your name when you decide its time to "connect" with them on your subject.

Then courtesy and respect.

State political credibility: You must establish credibility. To get this started you must know your subject inside and out. It will develop quickly if you have the answers, but, and it's a big but, no pun intended – do not guess or make something up. That will ice you forever with that person or persons and the word travels. If you don't know, say so. Tell them you will get the answers and then <u>follow through!</u> They will respect you for that.

If you are going to testify before a legislative committee, please get the names of the committee members, find out where they are from, then pick one, or two if things will be significantly different in your examples, and figure out how it will affect their constituents or districts.

In your brief, as possible, testimony give those examples. "Senator Jane, in you district this will be a cost savings of, or definite benefit for your constituents along the river highway " or whatever.

This is a lot of work most times but it can produce extremely positive results. It won't hurt to have analyzed all the committee members situation in case they ask questions of you. This saves them lots of time calling, researching etc. They will probably check on your figures the first time or some might and tell others, so you must be right. If you are, you have just advanced your cause considerably and established your credibility at an unreasonably high level setting you up for future successes.

Federal Go out of your way to make personal contact with your Senators and Congressmen. Go to their listening sessions. Give them short, concise, accurate input. They will soon call on you by name when you hold your hand up. Think about the presidential press conferences. He calls on the ones by name that he can trust – the others go unnoticed. Its good to know your elected officials, but that's not where you get the job done. The job is done by the staffers. Find the staffer who deals with your subject, Treat them with respect and courtesy, give them plenty of accurate data to support your cause. Trust me, most elected officials depend on them.

The young "kids" you see running around the Senators office are running this country. They write the legislation, they tell the Senator what's in it, and how it affects his or her constituency and they tell them how to vote on it, and most other legislation.

Let me give you another example of the kids running this country. A few years ago I had the opportunity to accompany the Air Force on KC135R refueling plane to Vandenburg Air Force Base in California to watch them test fire a minute man three missile. We were getting ready to leave Malmstrom Air Force Base in Montana and we were all in the plane, That is about a dozen of us community "leaders" and this bunch of Air Force kids. They were helping us get situated and getting us drinks and snacks from coolers and they had set up card tables for us to entertain ourselves, etc. Well, its time to go and I'm thinking the pilots ought to be showing up. About that time a couple of the kids slammed and latched the door and a couple others jumped in the pilot seats and we were out of there!

Agency decision makers: Very much of the same but remember the political appointments are important, very important but temporary usually. Get to know the staffers that do the work. They will be there. You need them to help carry your credibility over between administrations.

Now credibility and longevity are important. You can do longevity two ways, either by individual or by organization.

I'm not a fan of mandatory term limits but either way be sure to elect or appoint reputable people as the chair or president of your orginization. Don't just put Susie or Joe in there because they have been there a long time and deserve it. Put whoever will dedicate themselves to do the job right. One weak leader dumps the longevity and credibility of your organization and you must start over.

An example I can give you of how we got the job done in Montana is the changes we made in how out secondary road program works. We were having problems with how our State legislated secondary program was working with getting projects funded. We had our Federal money split up 56 ways for the 56 counties. We accumulated money over the years by a formula till we could do a project. We would at times have 10-15 million dollars or more obligated and couldn't build a project because we all had 3 or 4 hundred thousand but no one had a couple million. We started formulating a bill draft solution right after a legislative session. Our legislature meets every two years for 90 days (some people think that should be two days every 90 years but anyway) between the Montana Association of Counties Transportation Committee, which I chair and the Montana Department of Transportation, we spent almost two years getting the legislation written. We then got it approved by 56 Counties and all Montana Department of Transportation people including, planning, legal and management.

We got a sponsor and the legislation went through without a single amendment. Unheard of for that major and complex of a bill but we had done out homework including overcoming all opposition we could find by fine tuning the bill draft, exposing most of the legislators to it when they were home at the County level before the session, and "Knowing" the bill so questions were answered quickly and honestly. Just move the "S" its work, but it works.

In closing, remember that you are dealing with humans. Treat them with the same courtesy and respect that you'd want if you were in their place.

After my presentation Sunday afternoon I went to the BBQ mixer get together in the evening. A professor from Texas A&M came to me and said he would like a copy of my presentation; I said, "I would too!" I then told him that I didn't have it written out but could do that when I get home and I would send him a copy if he would give me his card which he did then I did.

POINTS TO PONDER

Must you stand in before you can stand out?

CHAPTER 15
HUMOR

A Bit of Drivel (or Is It Snivel?)

After a few years of blissful marriage my wife figured out how to push all the covers off our bed onto the floor on my side. I don't know how she does this but I do know why. She enjoys the torture factor as she gets up and drags them back across my warm sleeping body at a speed that creates a rope burn on my neck. She obviously has a cooling system of some kind under the bed because as these covers come up they are at minus twenty-seven degrees centigrade. And she has an added touch of waving the covers as she pulls much like the motions she uses to clean a rug. It has much the same effect as fanning the door during an Alberta clipper. The combination of her actions turns my warm body into the color and consistency of a prune. She then crawls back under her warm preheated covers and begins to snore as I lay there with my eyelashes stuck to my eyebrows. Poor me!

Diagnosis

I was talking to my primary care physician during a routine exam. I explained to him that I just didn't seem to have it anymore. I can't seem to get my honey-do projects or much of anything else done. He said, "We'll draw some blood and you come back next week and we'll figure out what's going on."

When I returned the next week, I explained to the doctor that I was a grown up and could take the news in plain English. I don't need you using those six or eight syllable words that only you can understand! He said alright Vern, you're lazy. I said oookay, so now give me the six or eight syllable words so I can tell my wife.

Chlorine

On another occasion during the MACO mid-winter convention in Helena I was to address the group. I started it with the following:
I said that we small town rural folks suffered when attending these functions in the "big" towns. We are used to good spring fed untreated water. Here we leave the hotel bar at a reasonable time early in the morning, go to the room and everything is fine. But after a few hours sleep we get up and shower in the chlorine water and it turns our eyes red.

A few days later after voting for officers and board members there was a lull in discussion as the votes were being counted so I went to the mike and offered an update on the red eye situation. I said there was good news and bad news. The good news was everyone I had seen had obviously been showering but the bad news was that the red eye was becoming epidemic. I said that last night after leaving the bar and going to bed I had to get up to go to the bathroom.

I had made this trip so many times I knew my way without turning on the light. As I strolled through the bathroom I glanced at the mirror as I walked by and it looked like a set of taillights going by. When I got to the commode I looked down and there was a set of hazard flashers in the water. After the startle subsided I realized it was me doing the blinking!

Sleep

Sleep is not really good for you as it dumbs you down. Case in point, I was the smartest guy in the bar in the very early hours this morning and after only five hours of sleep I woke up not knowing a darn thing!

A One-Liner after a Report

I gave a report on the NACO transportation committee to MACO attendees and started with this bit of profound knowledge!

"I read that a scientist in a lab somewhere had discovered and then published an article stating that once you burn something you can't burn it again. Obviously he has never eaten leftovers at our house!!"

More Leftovers

We were in question of whether some black olives that had been open in the refrigerator for some time were still edible. Dana asked Google and the answer was "if they taste funny don't ingest them." I tried one and it didn't make me laugh so we ate them and they worked better than some laxatives we have used, so obviously they were still good.

POINTS TO PONDER

Must you step down before you can step up?

CHAPTER 16
MOVING ON AGAIN

Election Loss

In the fall of 2003 I had made the decision to run again in '04 for a fourth term as a commissioner. In September a News Argus staff writer that covered a lot of the meetings I attended asked me for an interview. I obliged because I knew him to be a fair shooter and when running for office publicity is usually a good thing. The interview went quite well and I awaited the article to be published. It was and is copied here in its entirety including their headline.

The article was accurate from the interview but the headline upset many, many people. Some didn't bother to read the article they just went by the headline and it stuck in their craw right through to the election and I was soundly defeated.

There very well could have been other contributing factors as I never, ever in the eighteen years made a decision based on how it might look or affect the next election.

I always based my vote on the facts as I had them and how it would affect the budget and the people of the county. I recall an occasion when we had a decision to make that certainly was going to be controversial. I was asked if maybe we should wait until after the next election as I may not be reelected. My response was that if we put it off for that reason I probably shouldn't be reelected. I was not a good "politician" in that respect. I watch that game being played in DC all the time and it still aggravates me.

As it turned out I was very appreciative of those that continued to support me at the polls but, although I didn't know it at the time, the other voters that didn't support me I owe a great deal of gratitude as well. We would not be living the life on the road that we have now had I been reelected. The income just wasn't there to support what we're doing now so thank you to all who voted for John!

Getting Things Done

Vern Petersen at his desk in the Fergus County Courthouse, piled high with paperwork. That desk indicates what a busy – and powerful – man he is. The chairman of the Fergus County Commission said he plans to run for re-election next year.

Photo by Jim Dullenty

He'd never say so himself, but Vern Petersen just may be the most powerful man in the county

by JIM DULLENTY
News-Argus Staff Writer

Vern Petersen, chairman of the Fergus County Commissioners, is, arguably, the most powerful man in Central Montana.

But when you tell him people think that of him, he just laughs, saying "It isn't true, I am just one of three votes."

Petersen's power, however, is not just as chairman of the Fergus commissioners where he does have just one vote. He serves on more committees, commissions and boards than just about anybody in the region and he is chairman of several.

And when people want something done, they almost always turn to the Fergus County chairman for help.

At a recent public meeting of the Fergus County Port Authority, one of the few groups of which Petersen is not a member, he was asked several questions about how to fund the port group.

The principal method of funding, several suggested, would be to put a two-mill levy on the ballot in Fergus County. But when Petersen, at the meeting, seemed less than enthusiastic about the mill levy, the proposal seemed doomed.

Petersen made those remarks at a meeting that began at 7 a.m. in the Yogo Inn. Before the day was over, Petersen had attended at least four other meetings and was chairman of two. The last meeting ended about 5 p.m.

But Petersen, self-deprecating as usual, noted the chairmanship of the county commission traditionally has gone to the person who is in the last two years of their term. Since he plans to run again when his term expires next year, if he wins, he might not be re-elected chairman by the other commissioners.

In a variation on the Abe Lincoln log cabin theme, Petersen, 59, was born in an old log schoolhouse near Sand Springs in Garfield County. His parents were ranchers and he has two brothers and a sister. His father, Carl, is living in Winnett.

"We were raised north of Mosby on the Musselshell River, on the western edge of Garfield County," said Petersen. "It was an old homestead my dad bought in the mid-1940s."

In 1956, he left with a brother to go to high school in Winnett.

See Petersen/page 10A

Petersen: '... a job that you can make what you want of it.'

From Front Page

The brothers batched in Winnett and he saw little of the homestead after that.

Following graduation in 1960, Petersen, at age 16, worked as a "roughneck" on a water and oil well drilling crew. The firm was Livingston Drilling of Winnett.

That lasted almost a year and Petersen went to work on a pulling unit in an oil field. That lasted three months. Then he went into highway construction and that lasted longer, from 1961 to 1982.

Petersen moved to Lewistown in 1962 and was married, in 1965, to the former Dana Jackson of Denton. They have four children and several grandchildren.

In 1982, the firm he was superintendent for, Wickens Brothers, was sold so Petersen went to work as a salesman for A. K. Equipment, an agricultural dealership in Lewistown.

He was there until 1986 when he ran for the county commission and was elected. He took office in January 1987, and is in his third term. He has served longer than the other two commissioners.

Never active in politics previously, Petersen said he ran for the nonpartisan office after being encouraged by two neighbors.

"I knew quite a lot about roads and since roads are a big part of our responsibilities, I thought I might do some good," said Petersen.

He's not sorry he ran and is enjoying the job "very much." He plans to run for a fourth term next year.

Petersen is active in too many groups to list them all, but a few will show the extent of his activism – and, some would say, his power.

He is chairman of Snowy Mountain Development Corp.; vice chairman and acting chairman of the Central Montana Resource Conservation and Development Area Inc.; president of the Central Montana Foundation; chairman of the District Six Human Resources and Development Council; chairman of the Emergency Snow Removal Counties, composed of nine counties; chairman of the Montana Joint Powers Trust; chairman of the Montana Association of Counties Transportation Committee; chairman of the Montana Association of Counties Property and Casualty Pool board; vice chairman of the Highways Subcommittee of the National Association of Counties Transportation Steering Committee; chairman of the Heath Rural Fire District; president of the Snowy Mountain Wool Pool.

Add to that membership of a lot of other boards, commissions and groups, not the least of which is St. Paul Lutheran Church of Lewistown.

"I've tried to be active and responsive to the needs of the people. This is a job that you can make what you want of it," said Petersen.

He said by being active out of the county and meeting the decision-makers, it has helped him serve his constituents.

"I work with our congressional delegations and I attend a lot of hearings at the Montana Legislature," said Petersen. "On the national level I'm involved with many national transportation issues."

You would think that as a member of all these groups and committees, as a long time county commissioner, Petersen would be viewed as a glad-handing sort of guy who back-slaps everyone.

But Petersen admits "I'm rather shy, I'm really a shy person."

He also has trouble remembering names, which is a big difficulty in his business. But there is no question about what Petersen says next:

"I do know a lot of people."

Safety Programs

In February 2005 shortly after my departure as a commissioner I was asked to speak to the LTAP convention/workshop at the Yogo Inn on why county safety committees/programs are a necessity. The following are my comments and a thank you letter:

LTAP MACO Loss Control Feb 05 Lewistown

When I got out of high school I was 16 and knew all there was to know about everything. I had spent my entire life in school and not knowing how long I would live I was not going to chance spending it all there so I got a job as a roughneck on a drilling rig. There was a crew of 4 on each 12 hour shift. They did not have a safety program. On my shift there was Lefty, Stub and Patch and the kid. They didn't have a first aid kit. They didn't need one because we didn't use band aids and such. You see if the wound wasn't losing enough blood to make the platform slick and dangerous you didn't fool with it. The bad injuries got a roll of gauze and what appeared to be white duct tape.

Lefty and Stub were very good to me and gave me a lot of compliments. They 'd say something like "we sure need to unload that load of drill stem today but we don't have time and the kid sure can't do it"! I'd be about half done and about to drop when I'd here old Stub say, "look at that kid go, I can't believe it, I'da bet money that no man alive could unload a whole load of drill stem by himself". Instantly I would have my second wind and speed up. It got so them two could work a 12 hour shift and not get their hands dirty. It was a good thing I was smarter than those two or I would have quit. After a year of that I got tired of all their compliments and did quit. I thought I'd find something where my peers would enjoy compliments as much as I used too. I got a job on a construction project building roads where I worked my way up to supervisor. They did have a safety program and I thought it had two primary purposes. One being to create a position for the minority running the program and the other to aggravate me and cost me production.

It's embarrassing to admit that now how wrong I was. You've got one licensed crane operator and he leaves at 8 am because he carelessly got hurt. Talk about loss of production   a laborer gets hurt, he knows your operation never wastes a step. It takes time and money to retrain. Then think of the actual costs of medical and rehab and on and on. Think of the loss of quality of life=-hardships on family-carelessness carries a huge price tag for both workers and employers.

So let me tell you why you need a safety program. I read where there was a study done recently and the average man thinks about sex an average of 4 times an hour. Now we're not talking commissioners and truck drivers here just average Joe six pack! I was a little surprised by that small number but I tend to judge on what I, never mind you know where safety came in? It didn't even rate a study!

So you need a safety program to remind all of safety every day or the only time safety will be thought about is right after the accident.

So you see I can sum it up in one sentence -You need a safety program because safety isn't sexy.

RISK MANAGEMENT PROGRAM

"SAVING$ THROUGH SAFETY"

A SERVICE OF THE MONTANA ASSOCIATION OF COUNTIES

2715 Skyway Drive
Helena, MT 59692-1213
PHONE: (406) 444-4370
FAX: (406) 442-5238
E-MAIL: macorm@maco.cog.mt.us

PROGRAM
MANAGER
RAY BARNICOAT

January 28, 2005

Vernon Peterson
HC 87 Box 5570
Lewistown, MT 59457-9312

Dear Vern,

We want to thank you for your presentation on the Importance of Having a Safety Program. As always, you are a natural entertainer who uses that skill to deliver a meaningful message that sticks.

Everyone was glad to see you. Stay in touch.

Sincerely,

Ray Barnicoat

Moving On Again to Another Chapter in My Career

I was not ready or in a position to retire after my defeat in the '04 election. Getting my pink slip notification in early November gave me time to look at my options. I talked to a couple contractors and found them very receptive to engaging in employment discussions. However I received a call from our third-party administrator for the Montana Joint Powers Trust that I had helped get put together back in 1988 and had been on the board ever since. I had been chairman of the board so I was acting as the administrator as a volunteer making the daily type decisions. He suggested that with my permission he would approach the rest of the board about hiring me to be the administrator. I indeed was interested and excited about the potential. The other board members were not heavily involved and didn't have the extensive background of the trust that I did so they were on board for the suggestion. I made up a job description and we held a board meeting and agreed on a salary and adopted the job description and made it official.

So I turned in my courthouse keys on the first Friday in January '05 and left for the last time. On the following Monday I started my new job and was off and running. My salary almost doubled and stress level was cut in half (or more). The only stress I had was what I put on myself in trying to increase the participation of more counties in the trust. Having served in so many MACO positions I knew almost every commissioner in the state along with all the clerks and recorders and treasurers and they knew me so that made my job and product very easy to relate to them. That effort was quite successful as we grew the lives in the pool by thirty percent the first year.

MACO had a worker's compensation pool and a property and casualty pool of which I had chaired the boards of directors. They decided a year after my employment by the trust to start a health care trust themselves. I was offered the administrator position for their new venture. I courteously declined the offer as I could not in good conscience go back to my clients and try to sell them on a new product in competition with the very worthy time tested MJPT. The counties had a good allegiance to MACO for lots of good reasons and with about a third of the commissioners changing every two years it wasn't but a couple years before we began losing counties to their trust. This made the decision we had made in 1991 to include schools in our trust look even better. This gave us a much larger playing field than MACO's so we were able to survive and thrive with the new competition.

With me being the only employee of the joint powers trust, I didn't get much vacation time. I was putting on about 50,000 miles a year traveling Montana and Wyoming. We had several groups in Wyoming including hospitals and cities and special districts. I also went into Idaho and checked with schools and hospitals but found little interest and it would have required some legislative changes so I didn't pursue there. I also visited western North Dakota with much the same story as Idaho so we didn't pursue that either.

In 2009 I was attending the clerk and recorders convention in the Hilton convention center in Billings. Cyndy Maxwell who I had worked with as she was clerk and recorder of Big Horn County was the president that year and I was really impressed with her people skills and outgoing personality.

I happened to be seated at a table next to where she was seated with other clerks having lunch when I overheard her saying she didn't want to run for reelection. She was ready for something different.

So the next week I called her and arranged a lunch meeting. She said she would love to go to work for the trust. I called a board meeting and presented my proposal of hiring her as my assistant. They were receptive so I came to an agreement with a job description and she accepted to start at the first of January 2010 when she would resign from her clerk job with the county. This made it possible to give our clients much more face time and to promote wellness efforts within the groups.

It also allowed me the ability to take a day or two off occasionally as well as spend a little more time in the office doing planning and bookwork during business hours rather that so much night work trying to keep up.

Hawaii

In 2010 the AGRIP convention was held in Oahu, Hawaii, so Dana took time off and went with me. After the convention we took an extra week and became tourists. A good friend of mine that used to shear our sheep went to Hawaii every spring and sheared sheep for a large ranch on the Big Island of Hawaii. He lined me up with the operator of the ranch ahead of time so we were able to rent the bunkhouse where the shearers stayed when they were there. After touring Pearl Harbor we flew to the Big Island and rented a car. We stayed at the ranch and drove the whole island. We went to an active volcano, then went down to the ocean where the volcanic tubes were draining hot lava into the water making huge plumes of steam and noise. Dana had the misfortune of falling on the pavement at one lookout breaking her glasses and creating skinned up knees and hands, but she was tough and continued to enjoy our vacation.

We flew back to Honolulu and after staying overnight we drove our rented Mustang convertible to the airport with the top down. When we landed in Great Falls getting home it was 14 below zero. What a shock to the system!

POINTS TO PONDER

Do you have to play empty before you can be playful?

CHAPTER 17
CHECKING OFF
THE BUCKET LIST

Putting Miles on the Motor Home

In 2008 we bought a motor home in anticipation of retiring someday. We weren't able to use it much but did take a couple trips as I would take my computer and phone along and do business wherever we were. This worked pretty well so in 2011 at our annual meeting I asked the board for permission to put my office in the motor home for a few months in the winter. Since we had Cyndy on the ground if a personal visit was needed they were willing to give it a try. Dana retired the summer of 2011 so she was able to attend some of my functions when she wanted.

We had our annual joint powers trust board meeting on the 3rd of December that year so I attended that then started packing. We left for Florida on the fifth of December. We got to Sheridan, Wyoming the first night and it was snowing and I was tired so we stopped at the rest stop. I called the highway patrol and asked if we could spend the night there as there was a sign saying no overnight camping. The patrolman I spoke to said yes we could stay as that would be much better that being stranded out on the interstate. The next morning it was an outright blizzard. Finally a truck pulled in coming from the south so I asked the driver how the conditions were on the road.

Oh, he said not bad, you won't have any trouble so we headed out. I know that truck driver was laughing all the way to the bathrooms thinking I'll never see that sucker again! The conditions couldn't have gotten any worse. It took us an hour and a half to get to Buffalo thirty miles away. I couldn't even see the guardrail most of the time. At one point I glanced out my side and thought, "Oh my gosh" we're sliding backwards. Turns out it was a semi very slowly passing us so it gave me the illusion that we were backing up. Not a good feeling at all!

We spent a couple hours in Buffalo then it cleared a little so we headed on south. We made it to Cheyenne that evening and parked in a truck stop for the night. The next morning when we awoke it was eighteen below. I hadn't put any water in the holding tanks but I did have a case of drinking water in the cargo bay so I thought I better get that up here before the bottles burst. I stuck my head in to grab the case and it was toasty warm in there. The furnace ducts run through the frame under there which provided plenty of heat. My learning curve was pretty steep but I was getting there.

We had an RV site rented in Flagstaff, Arizona and I couldn't get up to the park due to the ice and snow so I put Dana in the jeep and had her push me up the street. We stayed there a couple days and toured the Grand Canyon where there wasn't much parking space in the parking lots due to the huge piles of snow. We ran out of snow finally just thirty miles north of Phoenix. Pledged then to never leave that late again!

We made it to Florida and rented an RV spot as far south as you can get by road along the Gulf shore right on the water of the Gulf of Mexico on Chokoloskee Island for a couple weeks then went to Key West for New Year's weekend. I had rented an RV site about five miles out from Key West so I wouldn't have to wind up downtown with the RV. I had the site programmed into the GPS so all is well, right? Soon I see a sign that says entering Key West. I'm thinking wow the city limits must include the whole island—NOT! Suddenly we are downtown and it's a very old town so the streets are very narrow.

We came to an intersection that was a T so we had to make a right-hand turn. There was a car waiting to turn left and he was watching his front fender and motioning me on and holding his fingers about two inches apart. What he couldn't see, but I could, was the jeep coming up over the sidewalk and threatening a fancy street light pole. I was sure I was going to leave the hind fender right there but what can you do? It's tourist season, and the streets and sidewalks are packed so you can't just park and unhook so I just kept going. We then had to make the next three left turns which were a bit easier but it took us right down the last street next to the water where we met a small coke delivery truck. His mirror was just lower than mine so we were able to clear that and my mirror was probably four inches from the rivets on the side of his truck. Then we headed back out and came to mile marker zero on Highway One and continued on the same two-lane road as we came in on. Lo and behold about five miles out it has us turn right and here is the RV park right by the road. All we would've had to do is turn left there instead of going downtown.

When I went in to register there was a gentleman visiting with the clerk. The clerk asked me how my day was going so I gave him a short history of our misfortune and the other guy there asked me if my license plate read NO POWER. I said yes and he said they were on that last narrow street and were laughing at us wondering what idiot would be driving around down there with a forty-foot motor home. Hey, what can I say, it's me. No way would I leave home without the GPS but they sure are not infallible! We enjoyed the rest of our week there then returned to Naples for the months of January, February, and March.

I had to fly back to Billings from Fort Meyers in March on my dime to attend a renewal meeting, and then we drove home in April for the summer.

Working remotely did not generate any complaints from our clients so the board was happy with the arrangement and we were delighted.

Travels in 2012

So, in 2012 I scheduled things a little better and we left for Florida in early November to try to avoid a repeat of last year's roads. Good luck with that!! We took a different route going east this time so we could stop in Minnesota and see Charmin and family.

We got to Wibaux about dark and it was snowing hard. By the time we got to Beach, North Dakota the road was solid ice and visibility was next to nothing so we pulled into a truck stop for the night. By noon the next day there was lots of traffic moving so we decided it must be ok. It was still very icy but had quit snowing so at least we could see. There were numerous vehicles in the ditches and a pickup towing a trailer tipped over in the median after taking out a good stretch of guardrail. Fortunately I didn't have to make any sudden moves so the motor home held on tightly.

2013

This arrangement was working well but it was challenging for me. I was on the phone (hands free but still distracting) a good share of the days and at every rest area we stopped and I would check my email and sometimes it would take an hour or more to get and return communications and to get issues resolved. This was not a problem as I was getting paid to do the job but it sure wasn't a vacation either so at the annual meeting in 2013 before we adjourned I told the board I wanted to retire soon. I promised them I would stay until we got a good replacement hired and that I would remain available to them and my replacement until no longer needed.

I looked up an old friend who had been the account manager for our trust when he worked for our TPA and talked him into applying. He was hired and went to work in March.

We made plans to leave on the 1st of November so we scheduled dental and doctor visits near the end of October. Dana had some issues so they scheduled an echo stress test for October 30th. That gave her a week to study for the test—but oh no, she was too busy so she flunked the test! Her doctor scheduled an emergency appointment with a heart surgeon in Billings for the next day. We stayed in the RV at home and left for Billings early the next morning. They wasted no time taking her in even before all the paperwork was done. They ran some tests and the doctor came and told me they were doing surgery NOW! The surgery took a long time and a nurse came out about once per hour to give me updates. They kept her overnight and found the stents were not working but felt they may function with time so she was released at 10:00 AM. The surgeon gave me his cell phone number (which shocked me) and told me to call anytime day or night if things went south and gave us the all clear to travel so we hit the road getting almost to Bismarck that day. We got into our RV spot in Florida on the 10th of November.

2014

In March with the new JPT administrator on board leaving me somewhat untethered from my computer (although it did make the trip) we boarded a cruise ship in Fort Lauderdale and went to Aruba then to Colombia then through the Panama Canal which was a lifelong dream of mine. We stopped in Costa Rica, Nicaragua and Cabo San Lucas, Mexico where a friend and his wife, who winter there, picked us up at the pier and gave us an extensive tour of that area of the peninsula. What a treat that was. After that we docked in Los Angeles and flew back to Fort Lauderdale. By mid-August I had used up my vacation time and was done. Only an occasional call or text with a question after that, what a relief!

So after fifty-four years in the fulltime workforce, I threw out the alarm clock and we were free!! Yeah!

Well not quite free as we still had our home and fences to watch over and painting and staining and mowing and fixing and spraying weeds etc. so we traveled in the winter and worked in the summer.

We returned to Billings in May 2014 to check in with the surgeon. Much to our surprise he had retired so I called him on his cell. He answered on the second ring so we discussed our options. He said he had worked beside a surgeon at Kalispell regional hospital and that would be the only one he would recommend. We called there and made an appointment so we went home and mowed the lawn and headed for Kalispell. They ran tests and discovered there was no circulation from the three previous stents and that she had another artery ninety-five percent blocked so they opened it with another stent, kept her overnight, and sent us on our way. We had an extremely busy summer with a retirement party at home with a big BBQ with twenty-six guests and trips to Yellowstone Park and all school reunion amongst the many other adventures. Retirement fits us very well!

In October we left for Florida by way of Oregon where we were visiting with some of Dana's relatives after finding our way through the mazes called Seattle and Portland and me stating, "That's the last time I'm doing that," we got a call from Paul Petersen telling us that brother Don was diagnosed with stage 4 small cell lung cancer and could we come back. Of course we will, so we headed for Portland—again! We spent two weeks in Billings with them then Donny felt good enough that he wanted to go home. When they left to go north to Grass Range we headed south.

We flew back to Billings in December for a visit as Donny was not doing well. We rented a car and drove to Grass Range and spent several days with them, then through tears I hugged him for the last time as he passed away on New Year's Eve 2014. We flew back again in February 2015 for his memorial at which I made some comments including the bike wreck story mentioned previously.

Summer of 2015

The summer of 2015 was an extremely busy time for us. We had school reunions (fifty-five) for me along with lots of family visits. We did get a little bored about the first of June so we locked all of our keys in the jeep so that called for a trip to the farm by the locksmith! (It doesn't take a lot to entertain us anymore.) Also we had the spreading of Donny's ashes on Black Butte in July with all our family except two grandchildren present. We spent a week in Buffalo, Wyoming providing a place for Peter, our grandson, to stay as he trained high altitude running. Dana flew to Oregon to attend the memorial for her brother Jerry, who had passed away in February. We went to Big

Sky and met up with Dana's cousin Genell that she hadn't seen for sixty years. She invited us to visit her in upstate New York on our way to Florida.

In August Marlin and family came to stay with us at home while he had knee surgery and recuperated. That all went well and they left for their return to Uganda in mid-September.

We left shortly thereafter and went north this time. We stopped at the Kipp campgrounds and watched the elk bugling at Slippery Ann Game Range then on into Saskatchewan, Canada. We went east on through Manitoba, Ontario and Quebec. Quebec was a bit of a challenge as we neither one speak French and very few of them speak English. I did figure out some of the road signs, like upcoming construction warnings. They can take a perfectly bad road and make it almost impassable in a matter of feet or métiers or something! Our goal was to get to the Maritimes, Prince Edward Island, Newfoundland and Nova Scotia but the RV parks were closing by then and I figured they probably knew that climate much better than I so at the border of New Brunswick we spent a night in a Wal-Mart parking lot and turned south the next morning. We spent time in Maine then on to Massachusetts, Connecticut, and Rhode Island then into upstate New York.

We parked at Dana's cousin Genell's place and toured that area. She took us down to NYC and we spent about a week with her in her Columbia University apartment as she guided us all over the city, including visits to the Statue of Liberty, Ellis Island, the 9/11 Memorial and Freedom Tower, Times Square, a Broadway play and so much more. We returned up through New Jersey and toured West Point Academy on our way back upstate. What a once in a lifetime experience we had that would have never happened on our own. (Thank you, Genell.)

We hit all the New England states and the rest of the eastern states spending time in Virginia including driving much of the Skyline Drive highway across the top of the Blue Ridge Mountains above the Shenandoah Valley, getting back to Florida in early November. At this point we have each been in forty-nine states. I'm missing Indiana and Dana hasn't been to Nevada.

We spent time in St. Augustine, Cape Canaveral and the Kennedy Space Center on the East Coast then west back to the same RV resort as last year.

After a little set up and leisure time we took a cruise in the Caribbean. We hit ports and spent time touring in Roatan, Honduras; Belize City, Belize; Costa Maya, Mexico where I rode the zip line across the bay (twice) so that's off my bucket list; and Cozumel, Mexico where we spent our fiftieth wedding anniversary on Dec 11th swimming with the dolphins, wow what an experience that was!

2016

We left for Montana about the first of May 2016 and had another very busy and enjoyable summer. We did a lot of visiting along the way including meeting with a former pastor from our home church and his wife in Indiana so I now have all fifty states visited. We did put in a small garden at home since we had to check in weekly (or so) to mow the lawns. We did a considerable amount of travel in Montana and North Dakota.

We left early in September and spent a week in West Yellowstone with Dana's sister Bette and husband Don at their time-share while we toured Yellowstone Park and attended a football game in Ennis that grandson Carson was playing in.

We then went to Utah and spent two weeks touring state and national parks. Very beautiful country that I didn't know existed. We went to Arizona and walked the skywalk over the Grand Canyon then went through Nevada (Dana's fiftieth state) so we got that goal checked off our bucket list!

We went to California to tour Death Valley. I had rented an RV site not far from an entrance to the valley and plugged it into the infamous GPS. We went by a park and Dana said I wonder if that's our spot. I said no, the GPS says we turn left in three miles and besides the sign says "trailer park." We found the left turn and proceeded over a mountain pass and into Death Valley. We got another four or five miles and the GPS said, "You have reached your destination on the right." Nothing but sand and rocks as far as we could see! It was a narrow, paved road with dry sand on both sides so I had to unhook the jeep and jockey about ten times to get turned around without getting the rear wheels off the oil or I would have been stuck. So after rehooking we traveled back over the mountain and pulled into the trailer park and lo and behold they had a reservation for us, imagine that! So after all that trauma and aggravation I had to spend the night with the copilot and all her snide comments.

We headed east and visited friends in Arizona and relatives in Tennessee and in Alabama on our way to Bradenton for the winter again.

POINTS TO PONDER

Do you need to work in before you can work out?

CHAPTER 18
MORE MILES ON THE MOTOR HOME

The following are excerpts from the road as we toured the US in our motor home:

2017

We headed north again the first week of May and the first couple days were pretty uneventful.

The third day we did have a bit of an adventure (my description, the copilot's is somewhat different). My plan (or lack thereof) was to go generally north in Louisiana into Arkansas to Fort Smith (small dot on the map with an RV park). The roads looked a little sketchy on the map but the GPS said it could get us there. I think it assumed we were driving a Humvee not an RV. Anyway there was no grass growing up in the middle of the road so I thought things were going ok albeit mighty slow. The copilot was getting somewhat restless and vocal so I spotted an antique shop and pulled in (a mutiny prevention technique I have developed) and she found a small treasure of some sort and talked them down to fifty cents so it was a fine investment and it calmed things down for awhile!

We ended up in four states instead of the two as we were in Louisiana, Texas for awhile, then Arkansas, then Oklahoma, and then back into Arkansas. And there's no mountains "back east," right? Wrong! We had one stretch of three miles of ten-foot-wide driving lane with a ten percent downgrade with many twenty mile an hour curves that lasted so long we would have merged with the road we had just came over except we were probably 1,000 feet below there.

The copilot had been complaining of reoccurring nightmares so I thought this would give her some new material to work with. Once again however the gratitude for my thoughtfulness has not been forthcoming as one would expect.

Anyway, we finally hit a real road and got to the small dot on the map which had eight exits. They should update the map with a larger dot. Only took nine and a half hours to go 316 miles.

Next was north toward Kansas City to connect with I-70 West. We stopped in Kansas to visit relatives and in Colorado then home to start mowing again. We didn't spend a lot of time at home as we traveled to Minnesota for graduation, then went up to Highway 2 and visited relatives and friends on the way back. We also went to Medora, North Dakota for sightseeing and a play along with many side trips. One of those was to Fort Peck where we spent a week sightseeing and attending a live play of *GREASE* in the old theater.

The Fate of the Old Homestead

We had a tragedy during the summer when a strong thunderstorm went through on the lower Musselshell River. Many years ago, Congress couldn't get consensus to pass a "wilderness" bill, so they simply went around the law and created a whole lot of "wilderness study area" which made all those areas to be treated as wilderness and had no time limit so they can "study" them into perpetuity.

So lightning struck in one of these areas near Fort Peck Lake. Being a study area, people were not allowed in to suppress the fire. By the time it burned out of the "area" it was huge and out of control. It burned all the way up to our old homestead and burned every bit of the place including all the old buildings and most all the fences. It went right on jumping Highway 200 and burned the place where I was born. It burned over 270,000 acres.

We toured the area before leaving and saw the devastation. It was very difficult for me to see nothing left where I was raised. Brother Larry also lost about twenty-four miles of fence lines. Thanks, Congress for your malfeasance and ineptitude on land "management!"

Late 2017

We left for the winter again in September touring some in North Dakota, visiting Charmin and family in Minnesota then to Iowa where we toured John Wayne's birthplace and museum. We toured the Bridges of Madison County then into Missouri where we visited the WW1 Museum and the Truman library in Kansas City and Independence.

We went on to Sedalia, Missouri for an International Newmar Rally. We spent ten days there then Charmin and a friend came to ride their bikes across Missouri from west to east and the trail came right by the fairgrounds where we were parked. I took them to their starting place then we moved to their next stop and gave them a meal and place to sleep. Dana followed me each day with Charmin's car so they would be able to leave from St. Louis for home. We did this all the way across the state winding up in St. Louis. We spent a day there touring St. Louis and the Arch.

After their departure Dana wanted to go north to Hannibal to tour Mark Twain's home and museum. I said "NO" not this trip as we've been in Missouri a long time, so the next day in Hannibal we toured Mark Twain's birthplace and toured the cave that he was lost in for three days when he was young along with several other attractions.

We went from there to Branson, Missouri where we spent three nights and attended five live shows. We went on to Florida from there traveling 3,312 miles from Montana in thirty-nine days. Not much visible damage from hurricane IRMA in Bradenton, just a lot of debris piles to be picked up.

We took another fourteen-day cruise in March in the southern Caribbean. There we spent time in the ports of St. Thomas, St. Johns, St. Kitts, Antigua, Martinique, Barbados, Trinidad, Curacao, and Aruba (again)—we love that island. On our return from Fort Lauderdale with the jeep we broke down and sat in the hot jeep without A/C for six hours waiting for a wrecker on Easter Sunday. We spent the night in Fort Meyers and the jeep was ready Monday in time for us to get back to Bradenton.

2018 and Cleaning House in 2019

We headed north again in May taking a different route out of Florida. We went up Highway 98 which runs along the Gulf shore, very slow but very scenic. We spent time in Pensacola where we watched the Blue Angels practice and toured their museum and met Dana's niece for lunch.

We stopped in Dallas and toured George W. Bush's presidential library. We also stopped in Oklahoma City for Daniel's high school graduation. We spent much time with family in June. We attended a Newmar international rally in Gillett, Wyoming reacquainting with people we met at other rallies and meeting new folks.

Finally during the summer we began the task of cleaning out over fifty year's accumulation of "stuff" from the house, some of which I don't think we'd seen for about that long. We sold a few things and took many a load to the thrift stores. It got to where they would lock their doors if they spotted me in time. We got about half done that summer.

After getting back to Florida we set up the RV and rested up then we flew to Barcelona, Spain for a cruise in the Mediterranean Sea. The cruise ship folks had a shuttle pick us up at the airport and we spent twenty-five days touring Barcelona, Spain; Toulon, France; Livorno, Pisa, Naples, and Rome, Italy. We were able to meet up with grandson Dean at the Obelisk in Vatican Square and tour Rome with him. We then went on to Katakolon, Santorini and Mykonos, Greece; Kotor, Montenegro; and Ponta Delgada on the Azores Islands, Portugal. Then cruised back to Fort Lauderdale where we caught a bus back to Bradenton.

We were able to finish the house clean out job in 2019. We left a tremendous amount of things there. All the household furniture was there and almost all the shop tools and contents including the tractor and snowblower and got it listed with a realtor in the fall before we left. We agreed that if the buyer didn't want some of the things they (the realty firm) would auction off the unwanted stuff.

We went east this trip visiting Charmin and family then on to Syracuse, New York for an International Newmar Rally. We enjoyed a week there then backtracked to Niagara Falls for a couple days touring both the American side and the Canadian side. We enjoyed absolutely stunning views on both sides. Went on to Gaffney, South Carolina and spent time getting some preventive maintenance on the Freightliner chassis of the motor home and touring their assembly lines. That was very interesting as they build many different chassis for school busses, UPS trucks, motor homes, over the road tractors, and more. They actually drive the chassis out of the factory when done.

2020

Here's a report I sent to the kids in April:

> We are doing well and nothing else. Although yesterday was an exception, we drove over to a park and drove around with about 1500 other cars for a little more than an hour and finally got our first covid "shot".
>
> Mom was looking on her phone while we were driving around, already with some anxiety, and reading about others who had received it already and what their experiences were, adding to our suspense. Obviously the shot has lots of possible side effects. One had dry eyes, one had itchy eyes, one had teary eyes, others had bad breath, runny nose, constipation, diarrhea, loss of hair, ringing of the ears, dirty fingernails, and ingrown toenails and on and on so we became a bit concerned.
>
> I finally told her that I thought if we died in the next day or two from a gunshot wound it would be the fault of the "shot". No pun intended, well maybe a little!!
>
> So far I wouldn't know I got a shot if I hadn't been there and mom is doing fine. She

```
thinks she has a tiny bit of swelling but no
discomfort so I think we're home safe, thank
you Lord!! We hope round two goes as well.


Dad
```

Round two went every bit as well so with the two-week quarantine that left us one week to get our act together to head north the 1st of May. Back home the realtors had many lookers but no one brought their checkbook. We went back there in the spring of 2020 and parked the motor home in the driveway and stayed there all summer. With the Covid-19 thing going on we were trying to be careful even though we had two Covid shots as our doctor said he was afraid we wouldn't live through it if we got it. We lived in the motor home as the house was being shown regularly so we didn't want to mess things up in there.

So we spent the summer watering and mowing trying to keep things looking good and counting the cracks in the driveway.

I put the Traeger and one of the picnic tables in the RV shop behind us so we were able to BBQ almost every evening regardless of weather which made it very pleasurable.

Pacemaker

I had a pacemaker installed on Dec 14, 2020 at Manatee Memorial Hospital. The surgery went well but I did have to stay overnight. That's when I figured out why hospital stays are so expensive. Every time you fall asleep they pay someone to come and wake you up!

The device went right to work jumping my heart rate from 31 beats per minute to 70. My blood pressure was high all night so when the doctor came in to check on me in the morning I explained it to her. I said the pump has been idling along so not putting out much pressure then you supped it up to over twice the RPMs so of course it's going to put out lots of pressure. She said, "That has absolutely nothing to do with it!"

I guess I'll have to go back and get a new doctor degree or just let the doctors take care of it, probably the latter.

Good News and 2021 Travels

In January we got good news that our realtor had a potential buyer for our home place. After a flurry of offers and counteroffers with some sacrifices on our part we began the stack of paperwork. They had to sell their house to get the down payment for ours so they moved in early before all was final with a temporary rental agreement which added significantly to the stack of paperwork. We got everything done and closed in mid March so with them wanting to keep all we left there the pressure was off. So with mixed emotions we did not have to get home quickly to start mowing and staining, Whew!

We done our share of visiting along the way to Montana including Mother's Day weekend with Dave and family in Colorado then on to Billings where we spent several days then to Great Falls to visit Kelly and Chuck and get our mail that is being forwarded to them.

We then went to Minnesota to attend Mark's graduation party after stopping in Winnett for a couple days visiting friends and relatives. After about a week in Minnesota we returned to Lewistown and spent a few days visiting and driving out "home" to meet the new owners. Nice young couple with five children and enjoying their country setting. We have to admit even though it is what we wanted it was a little awkward to be guests in "our" home of fifty-four years!

Marlin and Lisa and Abigail came to Montana so we spent time in Winnett and they stayed with Aunt Diane and Uncle Skip for a couple days. We then went to Great Falls where they stayed with Chuck and Kelly with us in an RV park. We then went to Kalispell where we spent a couple weeks touring and fishing. Marlin and Abigail caught some nice sized lake trout on a charter fishing boat trip so we had a couple fish fries and we rode the tram up Big Mountain near Whitefish. We also got in a lot of quality "together" time.

They left for Michigan from there and we toured western Montana from Libby to Dillon with many stops between to visit many past commissioners I worked with as well as relatives. Got back to Lewistown in mid-July and camped at the fairgrounds, staying through the fair and really got to see lots of friends and relatives and attended four funerals. We began touring again from there spending a very enjoyable week in Helena visiting many friends from my commissioner days along with a couple from the construction days that I hadn't seen for about thirty-five years. We also had lunch with a nice couple that was our neighbors for several years at Heath.

We spent a couple more weeks in Billings getting more maintenance and visiting done. From there we started our trek back south into Wyoming and visited niece Staci & family, then to Colorado again to Dave's, and from there into Utah where we met up with Ben & Charmin and toured Bryce Canyon and Zion Park areas again.

When we left there we went through Arizona, New Mexico, Texas, Oklahoma, Arkansas, Tennessee, Mississippi, Alabama, and Georgia where we were able to visit two grandchildren on separate military bases, Dean training at Fort Benning and Carmen teaching at Fort Stewart.

They both drove down separately and joined us for Thanksgiving weekend. We went deep sea fishing in the Gulf and they tried parasailing and both really enjoyed. We had a Traeger turkey for Thanksgiving and a fish fry so it was a wonderful weekend.

POINTS TO PONDER

Do you have to slow down before you can slow up?
Or do you have to slow up before you can slow down?

IN CLOSING...

WELL, THAT PRETTY much sums up our lives to this point. We have gravesites in Central Montana Memorial Gardens including headstones next to my parents' graves where we will be buried when that time comes. We have a prepaid contract with Creel Funeral Home of Lewistown for our services so everything should be covered. Better to be prepared and not need it than to need it and not be prepared!

As you have read, much of my life has been centered around "roads." I didn't know it at the time, but in a way, I was helping build roads when as young as five years old by riding in the wagon and walking and riding on the bike, wearing away the sagebrush to establish the two track roads we had then, even before seeing the bulldozer making a real road in 1954.

As noted, when I wasn't building roads, I was using them. I don't know how many miles I have driven but I did wear out five new pickups with well over 100,000 miles each during my construction days, along with several cars. As mentioned, I only bought two new cars in my life, but I also wore out many used ones as well. We have put a little over 100,000 miles on the motor home as well.

I am probably the only guy you know or have heard of that actually goes out of his way to travel through construction projects! I check the road reports and select the route with the most active construction going on. I enjoy seeing if the design is good and of course seeing if the contractor is doing it "right."

This reminds me of a time in 1963 when we were building a road east out of Ekalaka, Montana. We had an older, very boisterous mechanic/welder named Anchor that was very outgoing and vocal. He enjoyed a good argument. He would go to the restaurant early in the morning and when a couple he didn't know would come in he would engage in most any sort of conversation but he especially liked to engage in politics. He had an uncanny ability to engage others as well as enrage many. If he could get the man and wife arguing that made his day and accomplished his mission so then he could go to work.

One day on this job the head mechanic was gone on a parts run when a car with a Minnesota license plate pulled into our staging area where Anchor was working. The guy got out and asked Anchor who the head mechanic was. With him gone Anchor said, "I am." The guy said, "Then why don't you go up there and tighten the tracks on that D6 before you wear the idlers out?"

That was the only time I ever seen him speechless even briefly. I, however, have never been as bold as the Minnesotan referred to here, but I have been tempted.

I have had to back off the intentional construction routes while traveling with the motor home. In those projects dust is a problem, wet and slick is a problem, rough is a problem, and the copilot is a problem so I now have to avoid road projects when possible, darn it!

ABOUT THE AUTHOR

After a twenty-two-year construction career, Vern was elected to the office of county commissioner for Fergus County, Montana. While in office, Vern crisscrossed the state, making roads of all kinds as a transportation leader and later as president of the Montana Association of Counties (MACO). He served nationally on the National Association of Counties (NACO) as vice chair on the highways subcommittee. His childhood dream to drive bulldozers eventually led him to become a "roads" scholar.

Vern has enjoyed the journey alongside his wife of fifty-seven years, Dana, their four children, and eleven grandchildren.